McGraw-Hill's
JAPANESE
ILLUSTRATED
DICTIONARY

LïveABC

Mc Graw Hill

New York   Chicago   San Francisco   Lisbon   London   Madrid   Mexico City
Milan   New Delhi   San Juan   Seoul   Singapore   Sydney   Toronto

1 2 3 4 5 6 7 8 9 10 11 12 13 14 15 16 17 18 19 20 21 22 23 24 25 26 27 28 29 CTP/CTP 1 9 8 7 6 5 4 3 2 1

ISBN 978-0-07-176884-9 (book and CD)
MHID   0-07-176884-X (book and CD)

ISBN 978-0-07-176882-5 (book for set)
MHID   0-07-176882-3 (book for set)

Library of Congress Control Number 2010943205

CD-ROM and MP3 Disk
The accompanying disk contains recordings of all the entries in this dictionary, available in two formats.

1. MP3 files
These files can be played on your computer and loaded onto your MP3 player.
i.   Insert the disk into your computer and open via My Computer, or double click on the disk icon.
ii. Drag the disk icon "Japanese Dictionary" into your Music Library, or open the disk to access the MP3 files to copy to your computer.
iii. Sync your MP3 player with your Music Library.
iv. Locate the recordings under the artist name "Japanese Dictionary."

Note: if you allow your computer to "rip" or "import" the disk, the resulting recordings will not include the corresponding art and text for each dictionary entry.

2. CD-ROM
Installation instructions for PC
i.   Insert the disk into your computer and open the disk via My Computer.
ii. Double click on the "Japanese Dictionary Installer.exe" Adobe Air application.
iii. Wait while the program is "Getting ready to install this application."
iv. When the APPLICATION INSTALL screen appears, it will give you options for Installation Preferences and the location of the Study Player files (the default location is "Program Files"). Then click INSTALL.
v.   If you do not have Adobe Air already installed on your computer, a Warranty Disclaimer and Software License Agreement screen will appear. Read the license and select "I AGREE."

Once the program files are installed, the program will start automatically (if you checked this option), or click on the "Japanese Dictionary" desktop icon, or use the START menu and select PROGRAMS/Japanese Illustrated Dictionary.
No system modifications are made other than the file copy and program group processes described above.

TO UNINSTALL: Use the "Add or Remove Programs" tool on your Control Panel. The program to uninstall is called "Japanese Illustrated Dictionary."

Installation instructions for MAC
i.   Insert the disk into your computer. If the disk does not open automatically, double click on the disk icon.
ii. Double click on the "Japanese Dictionary Installer.exe" Adobe Air application.
iii. Wait while the program is "Getting ready to install this application."
iv. When the APPLICATION INSTALL screen appears, click INSTALL. This will give you options for Installation Preferences and the location of the Study Player files (the default location is "Applications").
v.   If you do not have Adobe Air already installed on your computer, a Warranty Disclaimer and Software License Agreement screen will appear. Read the license and select "I AGREE."

Once the program files are installed, the program will start automatically (if you checked this option), or click on the "Japanese Dictionary" desktop icon, or use the START menu and select PROGRAMS/Japanese Illustrated Dictionary.

TO UNINSTALL: Locate the "Japanese Illustrated Dictionary" in your Applications folder and drag it to the Trash.

If you experience difficulties, check the Read Me file on the disk.

Listen to samples of this and other Japanese language audio titles from McGraw-Hill at www.audiostudyplayer.com.

McGraw-Hill books are available at special quantity discounts to use as premiums and sales promotions or for use in corporate training programs. To contact a representative, please e-mail us at bulksales@mcgraw-hill.com.

This book is printed on acid-free paper.

Contents

Contents

We suggest that you listen to the audio recordings when using this book. It will make your learning more efficient.

Unit title in English and Japanese

Illustration with numbers

Category title shown in English

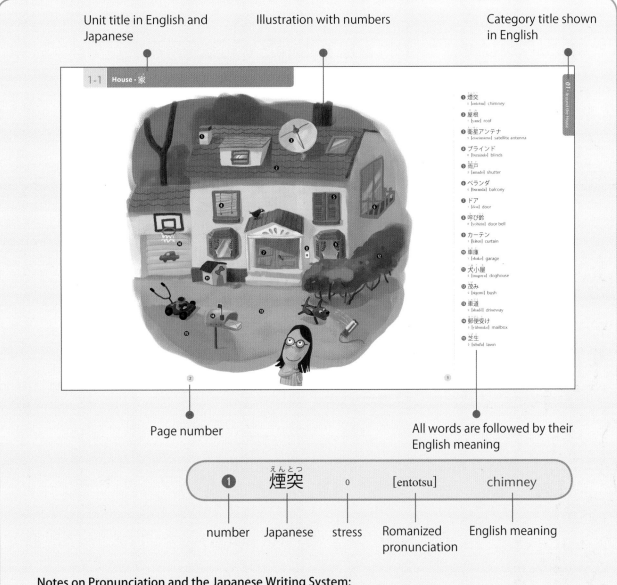

Page number

All words are followed by their English meaning

①　煙突　0　[entotsu]　chimney

number　Japanese　stress　Romanized pronunciation　English meaning

Notes on Pronunciation and the Japanese Writing System:

1. The vocabulary words in this book are written in either Kanji or Katakana, depending on common Japanese usage.
2. Words that are written in Kanji are accompanied by Hiragana script to facilitate pronunciation.
3. The numbers in red indicate stress. For example, the word "chimney" (えんとつ) is marked with "0", which means that the stress should fall on the last syllable "つ". If a word is marked with a "2", the second syllable of the word should take the stress. "1" indicates stress falls on the first syllable.
4. In the Romanized pronunciations, the sokuon（っ）indicates that the consonant following it should be doubled. For example, "husband" (おっと) would be spelled as "otto", with a double "t".
5. Also in the Romanized pronunciations, the mark "^" above a letter indicates a prolonged sound. So in a word such as "しゃどう" (shadô), the "o" would receive a more elongated pronunciation.

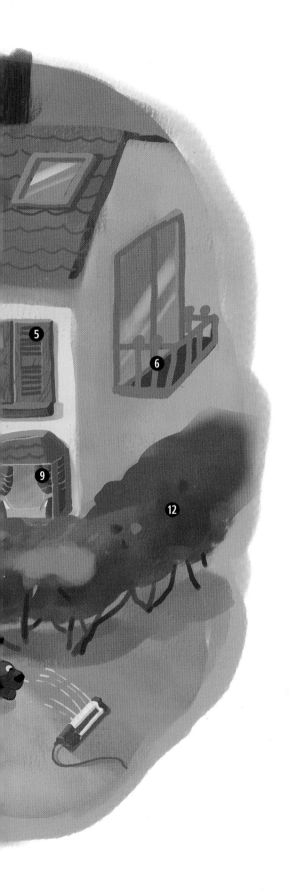

① 煙突
<ruby>煙<rt>えん</rt>突<rt>とつ</rt></ruby>
0 [entotsu] chimney

② 屋根
<ruby>屋<rt>や</rt>根<rt>ね</rt></ruby>
1 [yane] roof

③ 衛星アンテナ
<ruby>衛<rt>えい</rt>星<rt>せい</rt></ruby>アンテナ
5 [eiseiantena] satellite antenna

④ ブラインド
0 [buraindo] blinds

⑤ 雨戸
<ruby>雨<rt>あま</rt>戸<rt>ど</rt></ruby>
2 [amado] shutter

⑥ ベランダ
0 [beranda] balcony

⑦ ドア
1 [doa] door

⑧ 呼び鈴
<ruby>呼<rt>よ</rt></ruby>び<ruby>鈴<rt>りん</rt></ruby>
0 [yobirin] door bell

⑨ カーテン
1 [kâten] curtain

⑩ 車庫
<ruby>車<rt>しゃ</rt>庫<rt>こ</rt></ruby>
1 [shako] garage

⑪ 犬小屋
<ruby>犬<rt>いぬ</rt>小<rt>ご</rt>屋<rt>や</rt></ruby>
0 [inugoya] doghouse

⑫ 茂み
<ruby>茂<rt>しげ</rt></ruby>み
0 [sigemi] bush

⑬ 車道
<ruby>車<rt>しゃ</rt>道<rt>どう</rt></ruby>
0 [shadô] driveway

⑭ 郵便受け
<ruby>郵<rt>ゆう</rt>便<rt>びん</rt>受<rt>う</rt></ruby>け
3 [yûbinuke] mailbox

⑮ 芝生
<ruby>芝<rt>しば</rt>生<rt>ふ</rt></ruby>
0 [sibafu] lawn

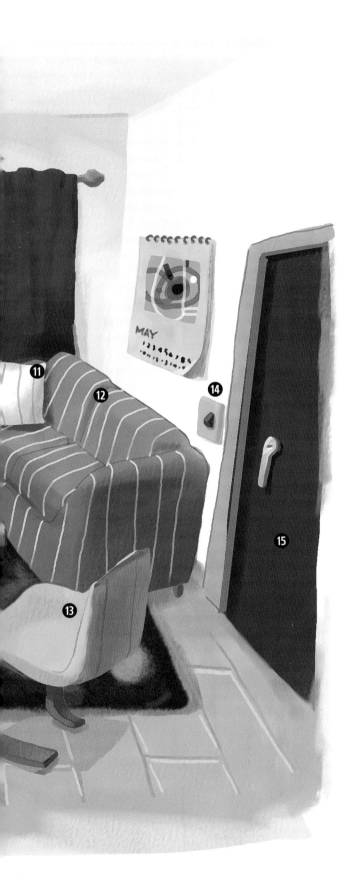

❶ 天井
<ruby>てんじょう</ruby>
0 [tenjô] ceiling

❷ 壁
<ruby>かべ</ruby>
0 [kabe] wall

❸ 時計
<ruby>とけい</ruby>
0 [tokei] clock

❹ 絵
<ruby>え</ruby>
1 [e] painting

❺ テレビ
1 [terebi] television

❻ 本棚
<ruby>ほんだな</ruby>
1 [hondana] bookcase

❼ 電気スタンド
<ruby>でんき</ruby>
5 [denkisutando] TV stand

❽ 床
<ruby>ゆか</ruby>
0 [yuka] floor

❾ じゅうたん
1 [jûtan] rug

❿ テーブル
0 [têburu] coffee table

⓫ クッション
1 [kusshon] cushion

⓬ ソファー
1 [sofâ] sofa

⓭ いす
0 [isu] chair

⓮ スイッチ
2 1 [suicchi] light switch

⓯ ドア
1 [doa] door

❶ タイル
1 [tairu] tile

❷ バスタオル
3 [basutaoru] bath towel

❸ 鏡 <small>かがみ</small>
3 [kagami] mirror

❹ タオル
1 [taoru] towel

❺ 洗面台 <small>せんめんだい</small>
0 [senmendai] sink

❻ 蛇口 <small>じゃぐち</small>
0 [jaguchi] faucet

❼ 石鹸 <small>せっけん</small>
0 [sekken] soap

❽ 歯磨き粉 <small>はみがきこ</small>
4 [hamigakiko] toothpaste

❾ トイレットペーパー
6 [toirettopêpâ] toilet paper

❿ コンセント
1 [konsento] electrical outlet

⓫ 便器 <small>べんき</small>
1 [benki] toilet

⓬ バスマット
3 [basumatto] bath mat

⓭ シャワーカーテン
4 [shawâkâten] shower curtain

⓮ シャワーヘッド
4 [shawâheddo] showerhead

⓯ バスタブ
2 [basutabu] bathtub

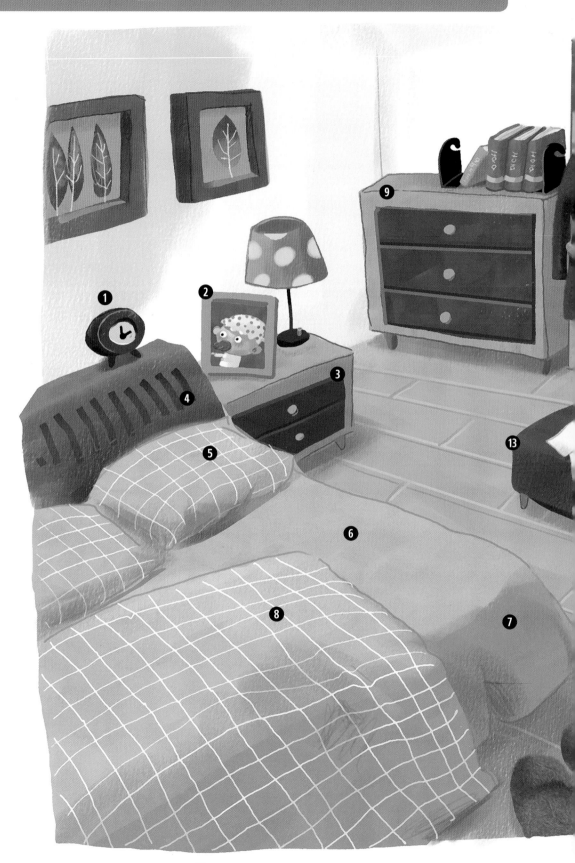

❶ 目覚まし時計
5 [mezamasidokei] alarm clock

❷ 写真立て
2 [shasindate] picture frame

❸ ナイトスタンド
5 [naitosutando] nightstand

❹ ヘッドボードキャビネット
7 [heddobôdokyabinett] headboard

❺ まくら
1 [makura] pillow

❻ マットレス
1 [mattoresu] mattress

❼ シーツ
1 [sîtsu] sheet

❽ 掛け布団
3 [kakebuton] comforter, duvet

❾ たんす
0 [tansu] chest of drawers

❿ 洋服だんす
5 [yôfukudansu] wardrobe

⓫ 化粧品
0 [keshôhin] cosmetics

⓬ 化粧台
0 [keshôdai] dressing table

⓭ 足台
0 2 [asidai] footstool

⓮ スリッパ
1 2 [surippa] slippers

❶ 縁側
  0 [engawa] veranda

❷ 障子
  0 [shôji] shoji sliding door

❸ 床の間
  0 [tokonoma] alcove

❹ 掛け軸
  2 [katejiku] hanging scroll

❺ 生け花
  2 [ikebana] floral arrangement

❻ 押入れ
  0 [osiire] closet

❼ 襖
  0 3 [fusuma] sliding door
(used to separate rooms)

❽ 畳
  0 [tatami] tatami

❾ 座卓
  0 [zataku] low table

❿ 座布団
  2 [zabuton] floor cushion

⓫ こたつ
  0 [kotatsu] Japanese foot warmer

⓬ 座椅子
  0 [zaisu] legless chair

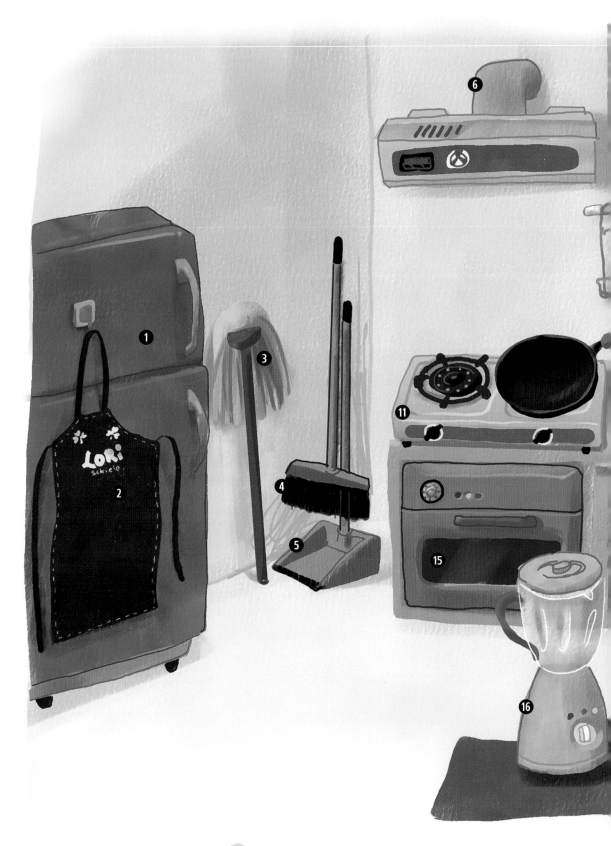

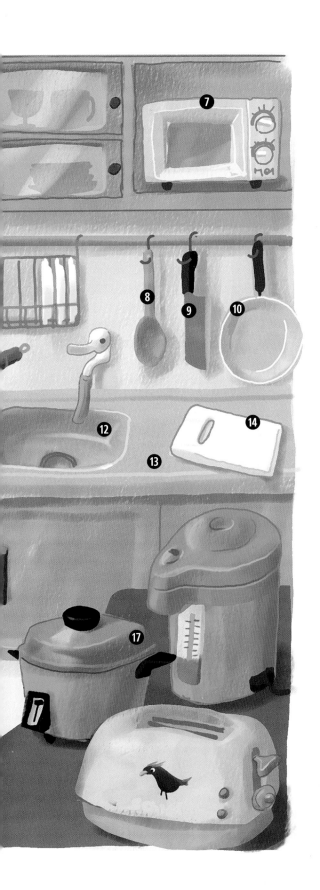

❶ 冷蔵庫
3 [reizôko] refrigerator

❷ エプロン
1 [epuron] apron

❸ モップ
0 1 [moppu] mop

❹ ほうき
0 1 [hôki] broom

❺ 塵取り
3 [chiritori] dustpan

❻ 換気扇
0 [kankisen] kitchen range fan

❼ 電子レンジ
4 [densirenzi] microwave oven

❽ お玉
2 [otama] ladle

❾ 包丁
0 [hôchô] cleaver

❿ フライパン
0 [furaipan] pan

⓫ ガスコンロ
3 [gasukonro] gas stove

⓬ 流し
3 [nagasi] sink

⓭ 調理台
0 [chôridai] counter

⓮ まな板
0 3 [manaita] cutting board

⓯ オーブン
1 [ôbun] oven

⓰ ミキサー
1 [mikisâ] blender

⓱ 炊飯器
3 [suihanki] rice cooker

❹

❶ コルク抜き
0 3 [korukunuki] corkscrew

❷ フライ返し
4 [furaigaesi] spatula

❸ ティーポット
3 [thîpotto] teapot

❹ ミトン
1 [miton] oven mitten

❺ マグカップ
3 [magukappu] mug

❽

❻ 栓抜き
3 [sennuki] bottle opener

❼ アルミ箔
3 [arumihaku] aluminum foil

❽ コップ
0 [koppu] cup

❾

❾ ラップ
1 [rappu] plastic wrap

❿ しゃもじ
1 [shamoji] rice spoon

⓫ 缶切り
3 [kankiri] can opener

⓬ ふきん
2 [fukin] dishcloth

⓮

⓭ 食器洗浄機
6 [shokkisenjôki] dish washer

⓮ 食器乾燥機
6 [shokkikansôki] dish dryer

❶ 掃除機
^{そうじき}
3 [sôjiki] vacuum cleaner

❷ ドライヤー
0 2 [doraiyâ] hair dryer

❸ 空気清浄機
^{くうきせいじょうき}
6 [kûkiseijôki] air cleaner

❹ ポータブル CD プレーヤー
9 [pôtaburuCDpurêyâ] CD player

❺ ヒーター
1 [hîtâ] heater

❻ コーヒーメーカー
5 [kôhîmêka] coffee maker

❼ ポット
2 [potto] hot water dispenser

❽ DVD プレーヤー
5 [DVDpurêyâ] DVD player

❾ ビデオ
1 [bideo] video tape player / VCR

❿ イヤホン
2 [iyahon] earphones

⓫ ヘッドホン
3 [heddohon] headphones

⓬ ステレオ
0 [sutereo] stereo

⓭ 洗濯機
^{せんたくき}
4 [sentakuki] washing machine

⓮ 衣類乾燥機
^{いるいかんそうき}
6 [iruikansôki] clothes dryer

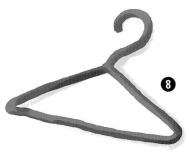

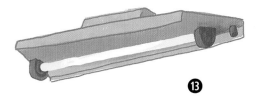

❶ 綿棒
　めんぼう
　1 [menbô] cotton swab

❷ シャンプー
　1 [shanpû] shampoo

❸ ボディソープ
　3 [bodisôpu] body wash

❹ 体重計
　たいじゅうけい
　0 [taijûkei] scale

❺ 爪切り
　つめ き
　3 [tsumekiri] nail clipper

❻ ランドリーバスケット
　8 [randorîbasuketto] laundry basket

❼ 洗剤
　せんざい
　0 [senzai] detergent

❽ ハンガー
　1 [hangâ] hanger

❾ ミシン
　1 [misin] sewing machine

❿ アイロン
　0 [airon] iron

⓫ アイロン台
　だい
　0 [airondai] ironing board

⓬ はさみ
　3 [hasami] scissors

⓭ 蛍光灯
　けいこうとう
　0 [keikôtô] fluorescent light

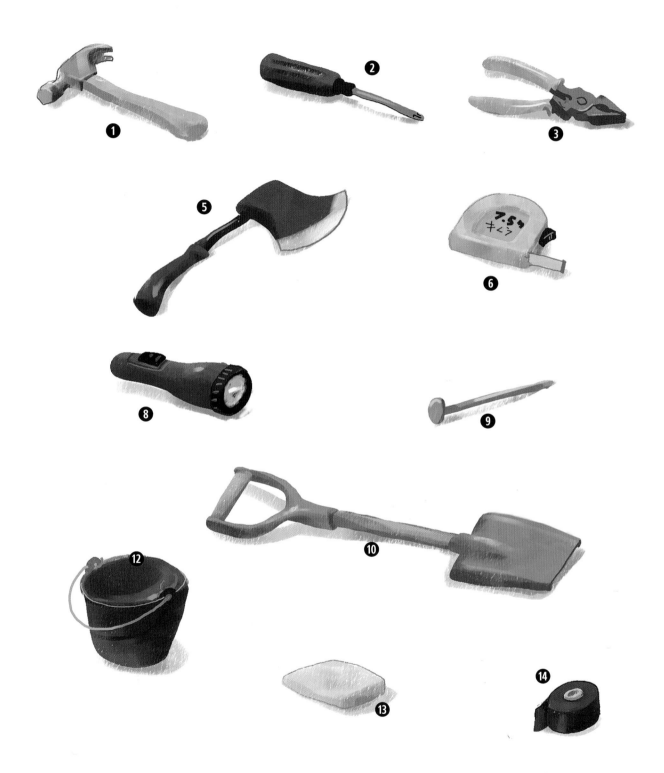

❶ ハンマー
1 [hanmâ] hammer

❷ ドライバー
0 [doraibâ] screwdriver

❸ ペンチ
1 [penchi] pliers

❹ ブラシ
1 [burasi] paintbrush

❺ 斧
<ruby>斧<rt>おの</rt></ruby>
1 [ono] ax

❻ 巻尺
<ruby>巻尺<rt>まきじゃく</rt></ruby>
0 [makijaku] tape measure

❼ 道具箱
<ruby>道具箱<rt>どうぐばこ</rt></ruby>
3 [dôgubako] toolbox

❽ 懐中電灯
<ruby>懐中電灯<rt>かいちゅうでんとう</rt></ruby>
5 [kaichûdentô] flashlight

❾ 釘
<ruby>釘<rt>くぎ</rt></ruby>
0 [kugi] nail

❿ シャベル
1 [shaberu] shovel

⓫ 脚立
<ruby>脚立<rt>きゃたつ</rt></ruby>
2 [kyatatsu] step ladder

⓬ バケツ
2 [baketsu] bucket

⓭ スポンジ
0 [suponji] sponge

⓮ ガムテープ
3 [gamutêpu] tape

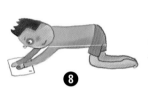

❶ 洗う
0 [arau]
to wash

❷ 掃除する
0 [sôjisuru]
to vacuum

❸ 掃く
1 [haku]
to sweep the floor

❹ 洗濯する
0 [sentakusuru]
to do the laundry

❺ 編む
1 [amu]
to knit

❻ 縫う
1 [nuu]
to sew

❼ 料理する
1 [ryôrisuru]
to cook

❽ 拭く
0 [fuku]
to wipe

❾ 寝る
0 [neru]
to sleep

❿ 目覚める
3 [mezameru]
to wake up

⓫ 歯を磨く
1 [hawomigaku]
to brush one's teeth

⓬ 顔を洗う
0 [kaowoarau]
to wash one's face

⓭ 食べる
2 [taberu]
to eat

⓮ 飲む
1 [nomu]
to drink

⑮ 着る
0 [kiru]
to get dressed

⑯ スカートを穿く
2 [sukâtowohaku]
to wear a skirt

⑰ 脱ぐ
1 [nugu]
to undress

⑱ 電話を掛ける
6 [denwawokakeru]
to make a phone call

⑲ タバコを吸う
0 [tabakowosuu]
to smoke

⑳ 見る
1 [miru]
to look (at)

㉑ 開ける
0 [akeru]
to open

㉒ 閉める
2 [simeru]
to close

㉓ 付ける
2 [tsukeru]
to turn on /
to switch on

㉔ 消す
0 [kesu]
to turn off /
to switch off

㉕ 入る
1 [hairu]
to enter

㉖ 出る
1 [deru]
to go out

1 男
_{おとこ}
3 [otoko] man

2 女
_{おんな}
3 [onna] woman

3 少女
_{しょうじょ}
1 [shôjo] girl

(少年
_{しょうねん}
0 [shônen] boy)

4 女の子
_{おんな こ}
3 [onnanoko] little girl

5 男の子
_{おとこ こ}
3 [otokonoko] little boy

6 幼児
_{よう じ}
1 [yôji] toddler

7 子供
_{こ ども}
0 [kodomo] child

8 赤ん坊
_{あか ぼう}
0 [akanbô] baby

❶ おじいさん
2 [ojîsan]
grandfather

❷ おばあさん
2 [obâsan]
grandmother

❸ お<ruby>母<rt>か あ</rt></ruby>さん
2 [okâsan]
mother

❹ お<ruby>父<rt>とう</rt></ruby>さん
2 [otôsan]
father

❺ おじさん
0 [ojisan]
uncle

❻ おばさん
0 [obasan]
aunt

❼ お<ruby>姉<rt>ねえ</rt></ruby>さん
2 [onêsan]
sister / sister-in-law

❽ お<ruby>兄<rt>にい</rt></ruby>さん
2 [onîsan]
brother / brother-in-law

❾ <ruby>妻<rt>つま</rt></ruby>
1 [tsuma]
wife

❿ <ruby>夫<rt>おっと</rt></ruby>
0 [otto]
husband

⓫ <ruby>弟<rt>おとうと</rt></ruby>
4 [otôto]
younger brother /
brother-in-law

⓬ <ruby>妹<rt>いもうと</rt></ruby>
4 [imôto]
younger sister /
sister-in-law

⑬ いとこ
２１ [itoko]
cousin

⑭ 甥
おい
０ [oi]
nephew

⑮ 姪
めい
１ [mei]
niece

⑯ 娘
むすめ
３ [musume]
daughter

⑰ 息子
むすこ
０ [musuko]
son

⑱ 嫁
よめ
０ [yome]
daughter-in-law

(婿
むこ
１ [muko]
son-in-law)

⑲ 孫
まご
２ [mago]
grandchild

① セールスマン
　4 [sêrusuman] salesman/saleswoman

② 配管配線工
　7 [haikanhaisenkô] plumber

③ 秘書
　1 [hisho] secretary

④ 運転手
　3 [untenshu] driver

⑤ ダンサー
　1 [dansâ] dancer

⑥ 歌手
　1 [kashu] singer

⑦ 農民
　0 [nômin] farmer

⑧ シェフ
　1 [shefu] chef

⑨ 俳優
　0 [haiyû] actor/actress

⑩ 漁師
　1 [ryôsi] fisherman/fisherwoman

⑪ パイロット
　3 1 [pairotto] pilot

⑫ 建築家
　0 [kenchikuka] architect

⑬ 機械修理工
　6 [kikaishûrikô] mechanic

⑭ 公務員
　3 [kômuin] civil servant

⑮ 大工
　1 [daiku] carpenter

⑯ 美容師
　2 [biyôsi] hairstylist

⑰ 弁護士
　3 [bengosi] lawyer

THE INTERNAL O

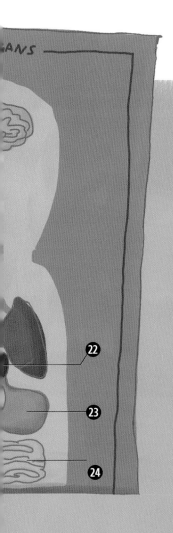

1 頭
3 [atama]
head

2 まつげ
1 [matsuge]
eyelash

3 首
0 [kubi]
neck

4 腰
0 [kosi]
waist

5 手
1 [te]
hand

6 尻
2 [siri]
bottom

7 足
2 [asi]
leg

8 髪
2 [kami]
hair

9 眉毛
1 [mayuge]
eyebrow

10 額
0 [hitai]
forehead

11 鼻
0 [hana]
nose

12 歯
1 [ha]
tooth

13 口
0 [kuchi]
mouth

14 あご
2 [ago]
chin

15 胸
2 [mune]
chest

16 腹
2 [hara]
belly

17 へそ
0 [heso]
navel

18 太もも
0 [futomomo]
thigh

19 脳
1 [nô]
brain

20 肺
0 [hai]
lung

21 肝臓
0 [kanzô]
liver

22 心臓
0 [sinzô]
heart

23 胃
0 [i]
stomach

24 腸
1 [chô]
intestines

❶ <ruby>喜<rt>よろこ</rt></ruby>ぶ
3 [yorokobu]
happy

❷ <ruby>元気<rt>げんき</rt></ruby>な
1 [genkina]
energetic

❸ <ruby>興奮<rt>こうふん</rt></ruby>
0 [kôfun]
excited

❹ <ruby>驚<rt>おどろ</rt></ruby>く
3 [odoroku]
surprised

❺ <ruby>怒<rt>おこ</rt></ruby>る
2 [okoru]
angry

❻ ばつが<ruby>悪<rt>わる</rt></ruby>い
1 [batsugawarui]
embarrassed

❼ <ruby>恥<rt>は</rt></ruby>ずかしがる
5 [hazukasigaru]
shy

❽ <ruby>微笑<rt>ほほえ</rt></ruby>む
3 [hohoemu]
smiling

❾ <ruby>笑<rt>わら</rt></ruby>う
0 [warau]
laughing

❿ <ruby>泣<rt>な</rt></ruby>く
0 [naku]
crying

⓫ <ruby>話<rt>はな</rt></ruby>す
2 [hanasu]
talking

⓬ <ruby>疲<rt>つか</rt></ruby>れる
3 [tsukareru]
tired

⓭ しりもち
3 2 [sirimochi]
to fall flat on
(one's) back

⓮ <ruby>跪<rt>ひざまず</rt></ruby>く
4 [hizamazuku]
to kneel

⓯ <ruby>蹲<rt>うずくま</rt></ruby>る
4 0 [uzukumaru]
to squat

⓰ <ruby>逆立<rt>さかだ</rt></ruby>ち
0 [sakadachi]
to do a handstand

⑰ 立つ
^た
1 [tatsu]
to stand

⑱ 蹴る
^け
1 [keru]
to kick

⑲ 背負う
^{せ お}
2 [seou]
to carry
(something) on

⑳ 体を伸ばす
^{からだ の}
6 [karadawonobasu]
to stretch

㉑ 歩く
^{ある}
2 [aruku]
to walk

㉒ 跳ぶ
^と
0 [tobu]
to jump

㉓ 座る
^{すわ}
0 [suwaru]
to sit

㉔ 転ぶ
^{ころ}
0 [korobu]
to fall

㉕ 寝転ぶ
^{ね ころ}
3 [nekorobu]
to lie down

㉖ 俯けになる
^{うつむ}
0 [utsumukeninaru]
to lie face down

㉗ 仰向けになる
^{あお む}
0 [aomukeninaru]
to lie face up

㉘ 這う
^は
1 [hau]
to crawl

FROZEN FOODS ❶ DAIRY ❷ BEVERAGES ❸ CANNED ❹

❽

FREE

SEAFOOD

❾

❼

❿ ⓫

FRUIT AND VEGETABLES

⓬

34

PACKAGED FOODS **BAKED GOODS**

❶ 冷凍食品
5 [reitôshokuhin] frozen foods

❷ 乳製品
3 [nyûseihin] dairy products

❸ 飲み物
3 2 [nomimono] beverages

❹ 缶詰
3 4 [kanzume] canned foods

❺ 包装食品
5 [hôsôshokuhin] packaged foods

❻ パン
1 [pan] bread

❼ 試食
0 [sishoku] free sample

❽ 肉類
2 [nikurui] meat

❾ 魚介類
2 [gyokairui] seafood

❿ 野菜
0 [yasai] vegetables

⓫ かご
0 [kago] basket

⓬ 果物
2 [kudamono] fruit

⓭ お客さん
0 [okyakusan] customer

⓮ レジ
1 [reji] cash register

⓯ レジ員
3 [rejiin] cashier

⓰ スキャナー
2 [sukyanâ] scanner

⓱ ポリ袋
3 [poribukuro] plastic bag

⓲ 現金
3 [genkin] cash

❶ びわ 1 [biwa] loquat	**❹ さくらんぼ** 3 0 [sakuranbo] cherry	**❼ ぶどう** 0 [budô] grapes	**❿ 柿**^{かき} 0 [kaki] persimmon
❷ すもも 0 [sumomo] plum	**❺ メロン** 1 [meron] melon	**❽ マンゴー** 1 [mangô] mango	**⓫ 梨**^{なし} 2 0 [nasi] pear
❸ いちご 0 [ichigo] strawberry	**❻ キウイ** 1 [kiui] kiwi fruit	**❾ 桃**^{もも} 0 [momo] peach	**⓬ レモン** 1 0 [remon] lemon

⓭ みかん
1 [mikan]
tangerine

⓮ オレンジ
2 [orenji]
orange

⓯ りんご
0 [ringo]
apple

⓰ グレープフルーツ
6 [gurêpufurûtsu]
grapefruit

⓱ マスクメロン
4 [masukumeron]
cantaloupe

⓲ バナナ
1 [banana]
banana

⓳ スイカ
0 [suika]
watermelon

⓴ パパイア
2 [papaia]
papaya

㉑ ドリアン
1 [dorian]
durian

㉒ パイナップル
3 [painappuru]
pineapple

❶ ねぎ
1 [negi]
green onions

❷ ピーマン
1 [pîman]
green pepper

❸ カボチャ
0 [kabocha]
pumpkin

❹ とうもろこし
3 [tômorokosi]
corn

❺ さつまいも
0 [satsumaimo]
sweet potato

❻ じゃがいも
0 [jagaimo]
potato

❼ カリフラワー
4 [karifurawâ]
cauliflower

❽ 里いも
0 [satoimo]
taro

❾ れんこん
0 [renkon]
lotus root

❿ マッシュルーム
4 [masshurûmu]
mushrooms

⓫ セロリ
1 [serori]
celery

⓬ にんじん
0 [ninjin]
carrot

⓭ なす
1 [nasu]
eggplant

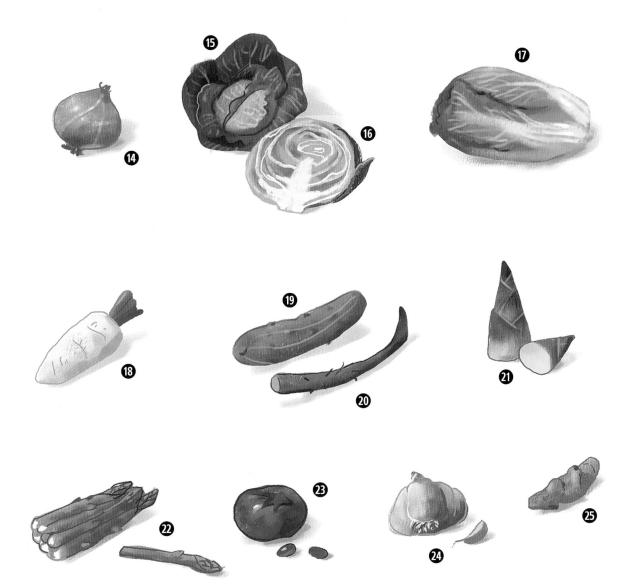

⑭ たまねぎ
3 [tamanegi]
onion

⑮ レタス
1 [retasu]
lettuce

⑯ キャベツ
1 [kyabetsu]
cabbage

はくさい
⑰ 白菜
3 0 [hakusai]
Chinese cabbage

だいこん
⑱ 大根
0 [daikon]
radish

⑲ きゅうり
1 [kyuri]
cucumber

⑳ ごぼう
0 [gobô]
burdock

㉑ たけのこ
0 [takenoko]
bamboo shoot

㉒ アスパラガス
4 [asuparagasu]
asparagus

㉓ トマト
1 [tomato]
tomato

㉔ にんにく
0 [ninniku]
garlic

しょう が
㉕ 生姜
0 [shôga]
ginger

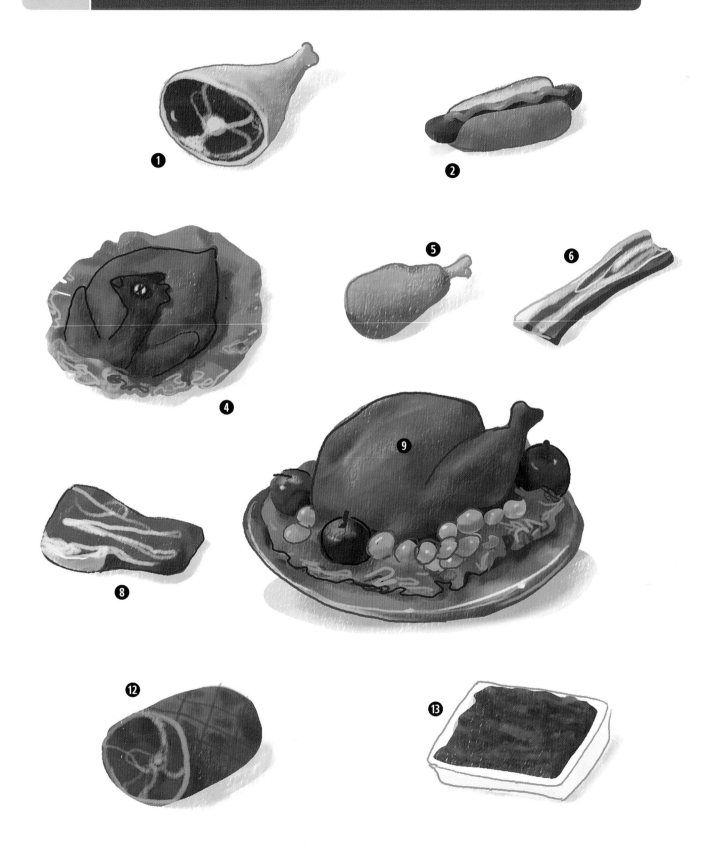

❶

❷

❺ ❻

❹

❾

❽

❶❷

❶❸

① <ruby>子<rt>こ</rt></ruby><ruby>羊<rt>ひつじ</rt></ruby>のもも<ruby>肉<rt>にく</rt></ruby>
3 2 [kohitsujinomomoniku] lamb shank

② ホットドッグ
4 [hottodoggu] hot dog

③ <ruby>牛<rt>ぎゅう</rt></ruby><ruby>肉<rt>にく</rt></ruby>
0 [gyûniku] beef

④ <ruby>鶏<rt>とり</rt></ruby><ruby>肉<rt>にく</rt></ruby>
0 [toriniku] chicken

⑤ <ruby>鶏<rt>とり</rt></ruby>のもも<ruby>肉<rt>にく</rt></ruby>
5 [torinomomoniku] chicken drumstick

⑥ ベーコン
1 [bêkon] bacon

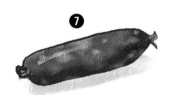

⑦ ソーセージ
1 3 [sôsêji] sausage

⑧ <ruby>豚<rt>ぶた</rt></ruby><ruby>肉<rt>にく</rt></ruby>
0 [butaniku] pork

⑨ <ruby>七面鳥<rt>しちめんちょう</rt></ruby>
0 [sichimenchô] turkey

⑩ サラミ
0 [sarami] salami

⑪ チョップ
1 [choppu] chop

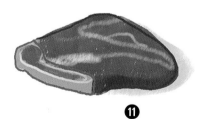

⑫ ハム
1 [hamu] ham

⑬ <ruby>挽<rt>ひ</rt></ruby>き<ruby>肉<rt>にく</rt></ruby>
0 [hikiniku] ground meat

⑭ スペアリブ
4 [supearibu] sparerib

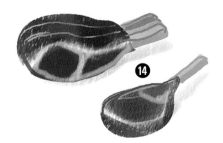

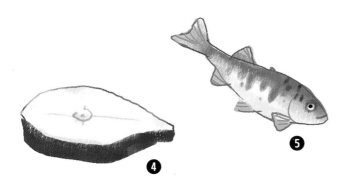

❶ ホタテ貝の貝柱
3 [hotategainokaibasira] scallop

❷ 車海老
3 [kurumaebi] prawn

❸ どじょう
0 [dojô] loach

❹ たら
1 [tara] cod fillet

❺ ます
0 2 [masu] trout

❻ 鯰
0 [namazu] catfish

❼ 鯉
1 [koi] carp

❽ ぼら
0 [bora] gray mullet

❾ あわび
1 [awabi] abalone

❿ 鰻
0 [unagi] eel

⓫ 鯛
1 [tai] sea bream

⓬ まぐろ
0 [maguro] tuna

⓭ 鮭
1 [sake] cod

⓮ さんま
0 [sanma] pacific saury

⓯ さば
0 [saba] mackerel

⓰ めかじき
2 [mekajiki] swordfish

⓱ かき
1 [kaki] oyster

❶ コーラ
  1 [kôra] cola

❷ 有機ドリンク
  <ruby>有<rt>ゆう</rt></ruby><ruby>機<rt>き</rt></ruby>ドリンク
  5 [yûkidorinku] organic drink

❸ コーヒー
  3 [kôhî] coffee

❹ アイスティー
  1 [aisuthi] iced tea

❺ ビール
  1 [biru] beer

❻ ソーダ
  1 [sôda] soda

❼ ミネラルウォーター
  5 [mineraruwôtâ] mineral water

❽ ホットココア
  4 [hottokokoa] hot chocolate

❾ ジュース
  1 [jûsu] juice

❿ ウイスキー
  3 4 [uisukî] whisky

⓫ ワイン
  1 [wain] wine

⓬ 牛乳
  <ruby>牛乳<rt>ぎゅうにゅう</rt></ruby>
  0 [gyûnyû] milk

⓭ 緑茶
  <ruby>緑茶<rt>りょくちゃ</rt></ruby>
  0 [ryokucha] green tea

⓮ スムージー
  2 [sumûzî] smoothie

⓯ 豆乳
  <ruby>豆乳<rt>とうにゅう</rt></ruby>
  0 [tônyû] soy bean milk

⓰ レモン水
  レモン<ruby>水<rt>すい</rt></ruby>
  2 [remonsui] lemonade

⓱ ミルクティー
  4 [mirukuthî] milk tea

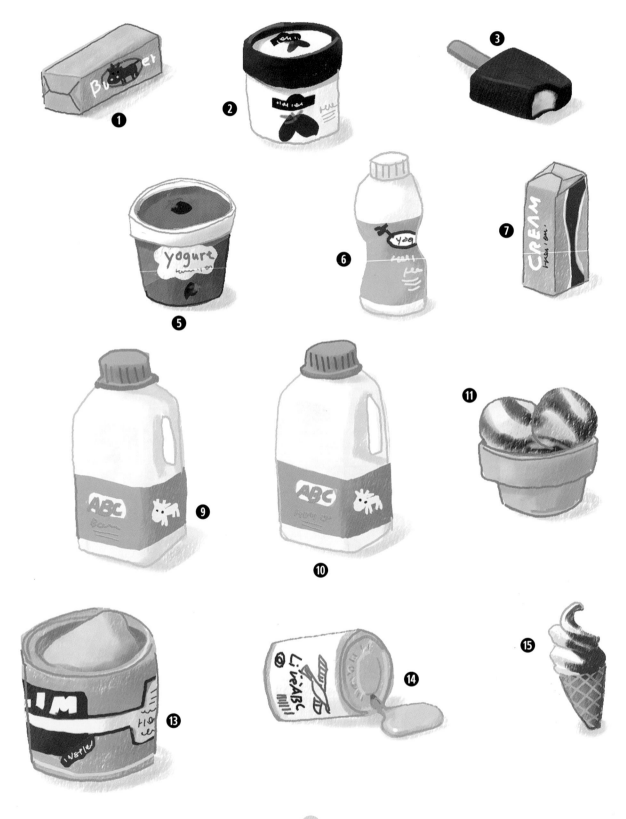

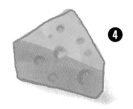

❶ バター
1 [batâ] butter

❷ アイスクリーム
4 [aisukurîmu] ice cream

❸ アイスキャンデー
4 [aisukyandê] ice cream bar

❹ チーズ
1 [chizu] cheese

❺ ヨーグルト
3 [yôguruto] yogurt

❻ ヨーグルトドリンク
6 [yôgurutodorinku] yogurt drink

❼ クリームチーズ
4 [kurîmuchîzu] cream cheese

❽ シャーベット
1 [shâbetto] sherbet

❾ 低脂肪牛乳
6 [teisibôgyûnyû] low-fat milk

❿ 無脂肪牛乳
5 [musibôgyûnyû] skim milk

⓫ アイスヨーグルト
7 [aisuyôguruto] frozen yogurt

⓬ ホイップクリーム
5 [hoippukurîmu] whipped cream

⓭ 粉ミルク
3 [konamiruku] powdered milk

⓮ 練乳
0 [rennyû] condensed milk

⓯ ソフトクリーム
5 [sofutokurîmu] soft ice cream

⓰ ミルクセーキ
4 [mirukusêki] milk shake

❶ 鉄板
　てっぱん
0 [teppan]
griddle

❷ 紙袋
　かみぶくろ
3 [kamibukuro]
paper bag

❸ ストロー
2 [sutorô]
straw

❹ チキンナゲット
4 [chikinnagetto]
chicken nuggets

❺ ホットケーキ
4 [hottokêki]
pancakes

❻ ドーナツ
1 [dônatsu]
doughnuts

❼ オニオンリング
0 [onionringu]
onion rings

❽ クロワッサン
3 [kurowassan]
croissant

❾ いす
0 [isu]
stool

⑩ ハンバーガー
³ [hanbâgâ]
hamburger

⑪ フライドポテト
⁵ [furaidopoteto]
french fries

⑫ トレー
² [torê]
serving tray

⑬ ベーグル
¹ [bêguru]
bagel

⑭ フライドチキン
⁴ [furaidochikin]
fried chicken

⑮ マフィン
¹⁰ [mafin]
muffins

1 カウンター
0 [kauntâ] bar

2 カクテル
1 [kakuteru] cocktail

3 ウエーター
0 [wêta] waiter

4 アイスペール
4 [aisupêru] ice bucket

5 シャンペン
3 [shanpen] champagne

6 ティーポット
3 [thîpotto] teapot

7 コーヒーポット
5 [kôhîpotto] coffeepot

8 ウエートレス
2 [wêtoresu] waitress

9 メニュー
1 [menyû] menu

10 コショウ挽き
4 [koshôhiki] pepper grinder

11 勘定書き
0 [kanjôgaki] bill

12 つまようじ
3 [tsumayôji] toothpicks

13 テーブルクロス
6 [têburukurosu] tablecloth

14 ランチョンマット
5 [ranchonmatto] placemat

15 ナプキン
1 [napukin] napkin

16 レジ
1 [reji] counter

① のれん
0 [noren]
shop curtain

② 座敷
3 [zasiki]
tatami mat room

③ 酒
0 [sake]
sake

④ 徳利
0 [tokkuri]
sake bottle

⑤ 杯
0 4 [sakazuki]
sake cup

⑥ 寿司
2 1 [susi]
sushi

⑦ お膳
0 [ozen]
tray

⑧ ラーメン
1 [ramen]
ramen

⑨ どんぶり
1 [donburi]
bowl of rice with
food on top

⑩ すき焼
0 [sukiyaki]
sukiyaki

⑪ 定食
0 [teishoku]
set meal

⑫ てんぷら
0 [tenpura]
tempura

⑬ 漬物
<ruby>漬物<rt>つけもの</rt></ruby>
0 [tsukemono]
pickled vegetables

⑭ 串かつ
<ruby>串<rt>くし</rt></ruby>かつ
0 [kusikatsu]
shish kebab

⑮ しゃぶしゃぶ
0 [shabushabu]
shabu-shabu

⑯ 刺身
<ruby>刺身<rt>さしみ</rt></ruby>
3 [sasimi]
sashimi

⑰ 割り箸
<ruby>割<rt>わ</rt></ruby>り<ruby>箸<rt>ばし</rt></ruby>
0 3 [waribasi]
disposable chopsticks

⑱ 箸置き
<ruby>箸<rt>はし</rt></ruby><ruby>置<rt>お</rt></ruby>き
2 3 [hasioki]
chopstick rest

⑲ 御絞り
<ruby>御絞<rt>おしぼ</rt></ruby>り
2 [osibori]
wet towel

⑳ 湯呑み
<ruby>湯<rt>ゆ</rt></ruby><ruby>呑<rt>の</rt></ruby>み
3 [yunomi]
teacup

㉑ おでん
2 [oden]
oden

㉒ 茶碗蒸し
<ruby>茶碗<rt>ちゃわん</rt></ruby><ruby>蒸<rt>む</rt></ruby>し
0 2 [chawanmusi]
savory egg custard

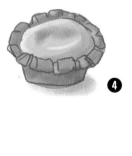

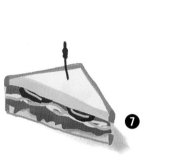

❶ ビーフステーキ
5 [bifusutêki] steak

❷ タコス
1 [takosu] taco

❸ サラダ
1 [sarada] salad

❹ タルト
1 [taruto] tart

❺ ローストチキン
5 [rôsutochikin] roast chicken

❻ アップルパイ
5 [appurupai] apple pie

❼ サンドイッチ
4 [sandoicchi] sandwich

❽ サンデー
1 [sandê] sundae

❾ チョコレートケーキ
6 [chokorêtokêki] chocolate cake

❿ 餃子
ぎょう ざ
0 [gyôza] dumpling

⓫ そば
1 [soba] buckwheat noodles

⓬ サブマリンサンドイッチ
9 [sabumarinsandoicchi] submarine sandwich

⓭ プリン
1 [purin] pudding

⓮ ラザニア
0 [razania] lasagna

⓯ チャーハン
1 [châhan] fried rice

⓰ スパゲティ
0 [supagethi] spaghetti

04 • At a Restaurant

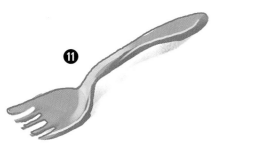

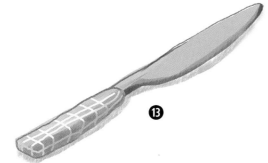

❶ 茶碗 ちゃわん
  0 [chawan] bowl

❷ はし
  1 [hasi] chopsticks

❸ フォーク
  1 [fôku] fork

❹ 大皿 おおざら
  0 [ôzara] platter

❺ 皿 さら
  0 [sara] plate

❻ ワイングラス
  4 [waingurasu] wine glass

❼ しょうゆ皿 ざら
  3 [shôyuzara] saucer

❽ スプーン
  2 [supun] spoon

❾ ティースプーン
  4 [thisupûn] teaspoon

❿ ナイフ
  1 [naifu] steak knife

⓫ サラダフォーク
  4 [saradafôku] salad fork

⓬ グラス
  1 [gurasu] water glass

⓭ バターナイフ
  4 [batânaifu] butter knife

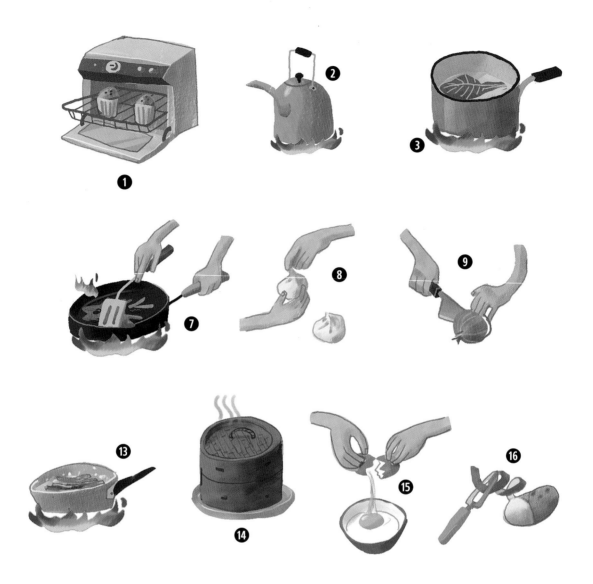

❶ 焼く
や
0 [yaku]
to bake

❷ 沸かす
わ
0 [wakasu]
to boil

❸ ゆでる
2 [yuderu]
to blanch

❹ 煮える
に
0 [nieru]
to be cooked

❺ 撒く
ま
1 [maku]
to sprinkle

❻ 刻む
きざ
0 [kizamu]
to chop

❼ いためる
3 [itameru]
to fry

❽ 包む
つつ
2 [tsutsumu]
to wrap

❾ 切る
き
1 [kiru]
to cut

❿ 混ぜ合わせる
ま あ
5 [mazeawaseru]
to blend

⓫ 挽く
ひ
0 [hiku]
to grind

⓬ 漬ける
つ
2 [tsukeru]
to marinate

⓭ 揚げる
0 [ageru]
to deep fry

⓮ 蒸す
1 [musu]
to steam

⓯ 割る
0 [waru]
to crack (an egg)

⓰ 剥く
0 [muku]
to peel

⓱ おろす
0 [orosu]
to grate

⓲ 薄く切る
4 [usukukiru]
to slice

⓳ 煮る
0 [niru]
to cook

⓴ バーベキュー
3 1 [bâbekyû]
barbecue

4-7 Seasonings・調味料

4

7

8

15

12

❶ 氷砂糖
4 [kôrizatô] rock sugar

❷ カレー
0 [karê] curry

❸ 塩
2 [sio] salt

❹ 胡椒
2 [koshô] pepper

❺ 鰹節
0 [katsuobusi] dry bonito

❻ 味の素
3 [ajinomoto] MSG (monosodium glutamate)

❼ バター
1 [batâ] butter

❽ 醤油
0 [shôyu] soy sauce

❾ 黒砂糖
4 [kurozatô] brown sugar

❿ からし
0 [karasi] mustard

⓫ 酢
1 [su] vinegar

⓬ ケチャップ
2 1 [kecchapu] ketchup

⓭ 油
0 [abura] cooking oil

⓮ 味噌
1 [miso] miso

⓯ 料理酒
3 [ryôrishu] cooking wine

1

2

3

5

6

7

9

10

11

❶ 辛_{から}い

2 [karai] spicy

❷ すごく辛_{から}い

2 [sugokukarai] very spicy

❸ まずい

2 [mazui] unsavory

❹ おいしい

0 3 [oisî] tasty

❺ 吐_はき気_け [~がする]

3 [hakike] nausea

❻ 甘_{あま}い

2 0 [amai] sweet

❼ 脂_{あぶら}っこい

5 [aburakkoi] greasy

❽ すっぱい

3 [suppai] sour

❾ しょっぱい

3 [shoppai] salty

❿ 苦_{にが}い

2 [nigai] bitter

⓫ さっぱりした

3 [sapparisita] light

⓬ もたれる

3 [motareru] to have indigestion

❶ 洋服<ruby>ようふく</ruby>
0 ［yôfuku］
dress

❷ ドレス
1 ［doresu］
gown

❸ ブラウス
2 ［burausu］
blouse

❹ スカート
2 ［sukâto］
skirt

❺ ストッキング
2 ［sutokkingu］
stockings

❻ ブラ
1 ［bura］
bra

❼ パンツ
1 ［pantsu］
underwear

❽ スーツ
1 ［sûtsu］
suit

❾ シャツ
1 ［shatsu］
shirt

❿ チョッキ
0 ［chokki］
vest

⓫ Tシャツ
0 ［tishatsu］
T-shirt

⑫ ポロシャツ
0 [poroshatsu]
polo shirt

⑬ ズボン
2 1 [zubon]
pants

⑭ ジーンズ
1 [jînzu]
jeans

⑮ 半ズボン
0 [hanzubon]
shorts

⑯ ボクサーパンツ
5 [bokusâpantsu]
boxers

⑰ セーター
1 [sêtâ]
sweater

⑱ コート
1 [kôto]
jacket

⑲ レインコート
4 [reinkôto]
raincoat

❶ かばん
0 [kaban]
purse

❷ マフラー
1 [mafurâ]
scarf

❸ ネックレス
1 [nekkuresu]
necklace

❹ ペンダント
1 [pendanto]
pendant

❺ ブレスレット
2 [buresuretto]
bracelet

❻ ヘアバンド
3 [heabando]
hair band

❼ 腕時計
3 [udedokei]
wristwatch

❽ 財布
0 [saifu]
wallet

❾ リュック
1 [ryukku]
backpack

❿ カフスボタン
4 [kafusubotan]
cuff link

⓫ ネクタイピン
3 [nekutaipin]
tie clip

⓬ めがね
1 [megane]
eyeglasses

⑬ バンダナ
0 [bandana]
bandana

⑭ コサージュ
2 [kosaju]
corsage

⑮ ブローチ
2 [burôchi]
brooch

⑯ イヤリング
1 [iyaringu]
earrings

⑰ ベルト
0 [beruto]
belt

⑱ 蝶ネクタイ
ちょう
3 [chônekutai]
bow tie

⑲ ネクタイ
1 [nekutai]
necktie

⑳ 手袋
て ぶくろ
2 [tebukuro]
glove

Hats and Shoes・帽子と靴

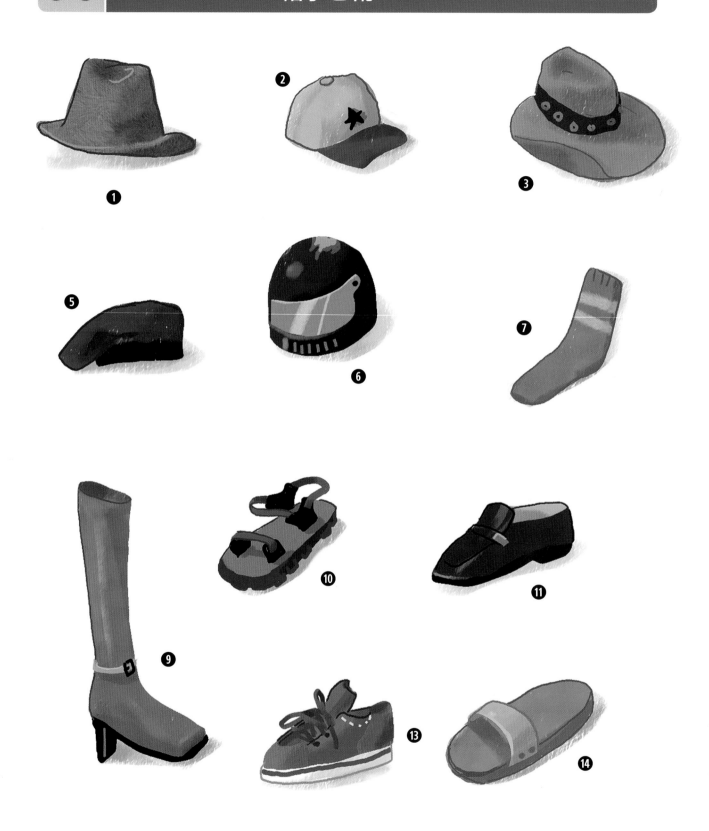

❶ 中折帽子
5 [nakaorebôsi] hat

❷ キャップ
1 [kyappu] cap

❸ テンガロンハット
6 [tengaronhatto] ten-gallon hat

❹ スキー帽
2 [sukîbô] ski cap

❺ ベレー帽
2 [bêrebô] beret

❻ ヘルメット
1 3 [herumetto] helmet

❼ 靴下
2 4 [kutsusita] socks

❽ 靴
2 [kutsu] shoes

❾ ブーツ
1 [bûtsu] boots

❿ サンダル
0 1 [sandaru] sandals

⓫ 革靴
0 [kawagutsu] leather shoes

⓬ ハイヒール
3 [haihîru] high-heeled shoes

⓭ スニーカー
2 0 [sunîkâ] sneakers

⓮ スリッパ
1 2 [surippa] slippers

⓯ フィン
1 [fin] flippers

05 • Clothing

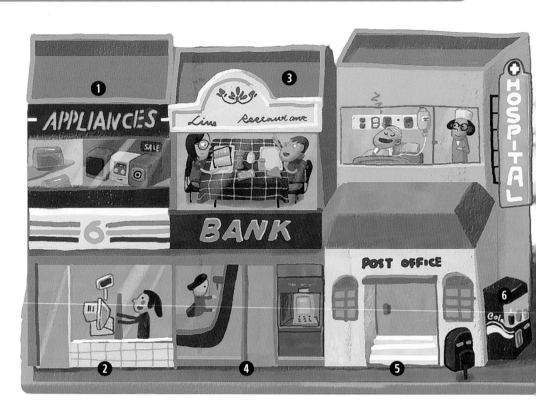

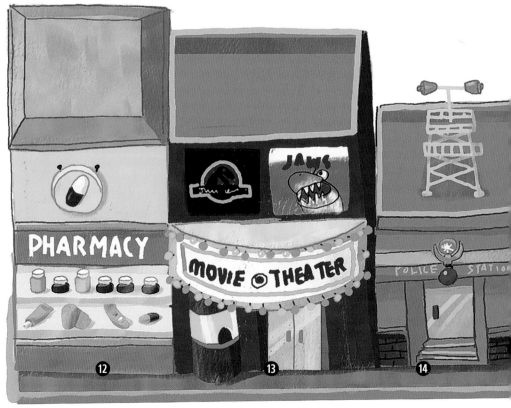

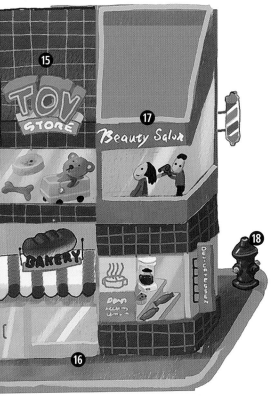

1 電器屋
　　〔でんきや〕
　　0 [denkiya] appliance store

2 コンビニ
　　0 [konbini] convenience store

3 レストラン
　　1 [resutoran] restaurant

4 銀行
　　〔ぎんこう〕
　　0 [ginkô] bank

5 郵便局
　　〔ゆうびんきょく〕
　　3 [yûbinkyoku] post office

6 自動販売機
　　〔じどうはんばいき〕
　　6 [jidôhanbaiki] vending machine

7 ホテル
　　1 [hoteru] hotel

8 家具屋
　　〔かぐや〕
　　2 [kaguya] furniture store

9 スポーツジム
　　5 [supôtsujimu] gym

10 本屋
　　〔ほんや〕
　　1 [honya] bookstore

11 新聞雑誌売店
　　〔しんぶんざっしばいてん〕
　　0 [sinbunzassibaiten] newsstand

12 薬屋
　　〔くすりや〕
　　0 [kusuriya] pharmacy

13 映画館
　　〔えいがかん〕
　　3 [eigakan] movie theater

14 警察署
　　〔けいさつしょ〕
　　5 0 [keisatsusho] police station

15 おもちゃ屋
　　〔おもちゃや〕
　　0 [omochaya] toy store

16 パン屋
　　〔ぱんや〕
　　1 [panya] bakery

17 美容院
　　〔びよういん〕
　　2 [biyôin] beauty salon

18 消火栓
　　〔しょうかせん〕
　　0 [shôkasen] fire hydrant

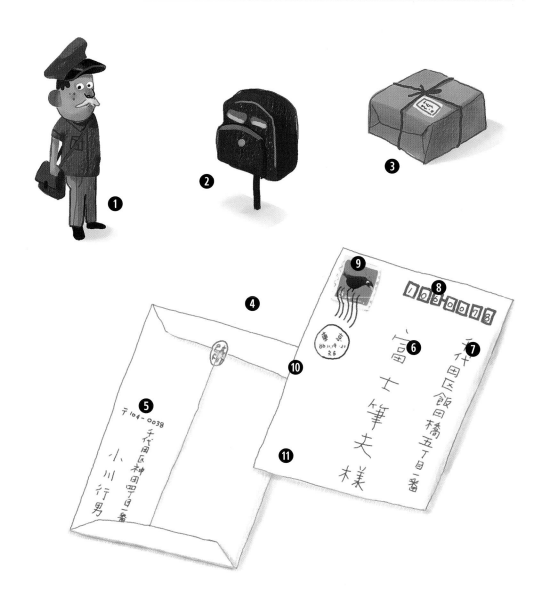

❶ 郵便配達員
5 [yûbinhaitatsuin]
letter carrier

❷ ポスト
1 [posuto]
mailbox

❸ 小包
2 [kozutsumi]
package

❹ 手紙
0 [tegami]
letter

❺ 差出人
0 [sasidasinin]
sender

❻ 受取人
0 [uketorinin]
recipient

❼ 宛て先
0 [atesaki]
recipient's address

❽ 郵便番号
5 [yûbinbangô]
zip code

❾ 切手
0 [kitte]
stamp

❿ 消印
0 [kesiin]
postmark

⓫ 封筒
0 [fûtô]
envelope

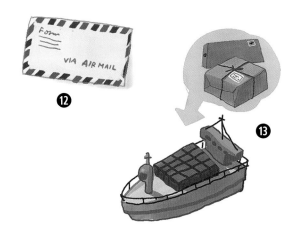

⑮

⑫

⑬

⑭

⑲

⑯

⑰

⑱

⑫ こうくうびん
航空便
0 3 [kôkûbin]
airmail

⑬ ふなびん
船便
0 [funabin]
maritime mail

⑭ は がき
葉書
0 [hagaki]
postcard

⑮ **E メール**
2 [îmêru]
e-mail

⑯ けいたいでん わ
携帯電話
5 [keitaidenwa]
cellular phone

⑰ でん わ
電話ボックス
4 [denwabokkusu]
phone booth

⑱ こうしゅうでん わ
公衆電話
5 [kôshûdenwa]
public telephone

⑲ **テレフォンカード**
5 [terefonkâdo]
phone card

① 警察署
5 0 [keisatsusho] police station

(交番
0 [kôban] police box)

② 刑事
1 [keiji] police detective

③ 交通警察
5 [kôtsukeisatsu] traffic officer

④ 巡査
0 1 [junsa] patrol officer

⑤ 笛
0 [fue] whistle

⑥ バッジ
1 [bajji] badge

⑦ 銃
1 [ju] gun

⑧ 手錠
0 [tejô] handcuffs

⑨ 警棒
0 [keibô] police baton

⑩ 警察犬
0 [keisatsuken] police dog

⑪ 白バイ
0 [sirobai] police motorcycle

⑫ パトカー
3 2 [patoka] patrol car

⑬ 通報
0 [tsûhô] to call the police

⑭ 消防署
5 0 [shôbôsho] fire station

⑮ 消防自動車
6 [shôbôjidôsha] fire engine

⑯ 消防士
3 [shôbôsi] fire fighter

WITHDRAWL

CURRENCY EXCHANGE

DEPOSIT

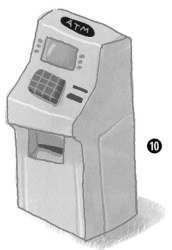

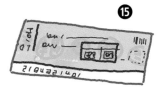

❶ 防犯カメラ
5 [bôhankamera] security camera

❷ 硬貨
1 [kôka] coin

❸ 札
0 [satsu] bill

❹ 金庫
1 [kinko] safe

❺ 貸し金庫
3 [kasikinko] safe-deposit box

❻ 引き出し
0 [hikidasi] withdrawal

❼ 非常ベル
4 [hijôberu] alarm

❽ 両替
0 [ryôgae] currency exchange

❾ 貯金
0 [chokin] deposit

❿ 現金自動支払機
1 0 [genkinjidôsiharaiki] ATM

⓫ 警備員
3 [keibiin] security guard

⓬ 現金輸送車
6 [genkinyusôsha] armored truck

⓭ 印鑑
0 3 [inkan] official seal

⓮ キャッシュカード
4 [kyasshukâdo] ATM card

⓯ 為替証書
4 [kawaseshôsho] money order

⓰ 小切手
2 [kogitte] check

⓱ 預金通帳
4 [yokintsûchô] passbook

❶ エレベーター
3 [erebêtâ]
elevator

❷ 売り場
0 [uriba]
shop

❸ 展示棚
3 [tenjidana]
display counter

❹ 店員
0 [tenin]
salesclerk

❺ 婦人服
2 [fujinfuku]
women's clothing

❻ 電気製品
4 [denkiseihin]
household appliances

❼ インテリア
3 [interia]
furniture

❽ ヤングファッション
4 [yangufasshon]
teen clothing

❾ 紳士服
3 [sinsifuku]
men's clothing

❿ 案内所
5 0 [annaijo]
information desk

⓫ 靴
2 [kutsu]
shoes

⓬ レストラン街
0 [resutorangai]
food court

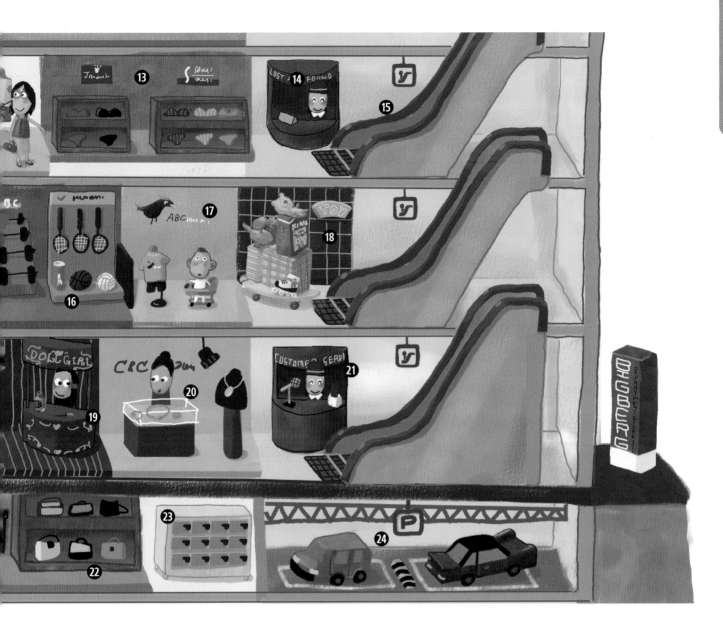

⓭ ランジェリー
1 [ranjeri]
lingerie

⓮ 遺失物取扱所
0 [isitsubutsutoriatsukaijo]
lost-and-found

⓯ エスカレーター
4 [esukarêta]
escalator

⓰ スポーツ用品
5 [supôtsuyôhin]
sporting goods

⓱ こども服
3 [kodomofuku]
children's clothing

⓲ 玩具
2 [omocha]
toy

⓳ 化粧品
0 [keshôhin]
cosmetics

⓴ 宝石
0 [hôseki]
jewelry

㉑ お客様相談室
8 [okyakusamasôdansitsu]
customer service center

㉒ 革製品
3 [kawaseihin]
leather goods

㉓ ロッカー
1 [rokkâ]
lockers

㉔ 駐車場
0 [chûshajô]
parking lot

❶ ジェットコースター
4 [jettokôsutâ]
roller coaster

❷ フリーフォール
4 [furîfôru]
free fall

❸ ボート
1 [bôto]
boat

❹ コーヒーカップ
5 [kôhîkappu]
coffee cup

❺ お土産売店
0 [omiyagebaiten]
gift shop

❻ 3D 写真
6 [surîdîshasin]
3D photography

❼ ライブショー
4 [raibushô]
live show

❽ バンパーカー
3 [banpâkâ]
bumper car

❾ パレード
2 1 [parêdo]
parade

❿ 輪投げ
3 0 [wanage]
quoits

⓫ 屋台
1 [yatai]
stall

⑫ お化け屋敷
- ば や しき
- 4 [obakeyasiki]
- haunted house

⑬ 射撃場
- しゃ げき じょう
- 0 [shagekijô]
- firing range

⑭ バイキング
- 1 [baikingu]
- pirate ship (amusement ride)

⑮ メリーゴーランド
- 4 [merîgôrando]
- merry-go-round

⑯ 観覧車
- かん らん しゃ
- 3 [kanransha]
- Ferris wheel

⑰ 軽食堂
- けい しょく どう
- 3 [keishokudô]
- snack bar

⑱ あずまや
- 3 [azumaya]
- arbor

⑲ ゴーカート
- 3 [gôkâto]
- go-kart

81

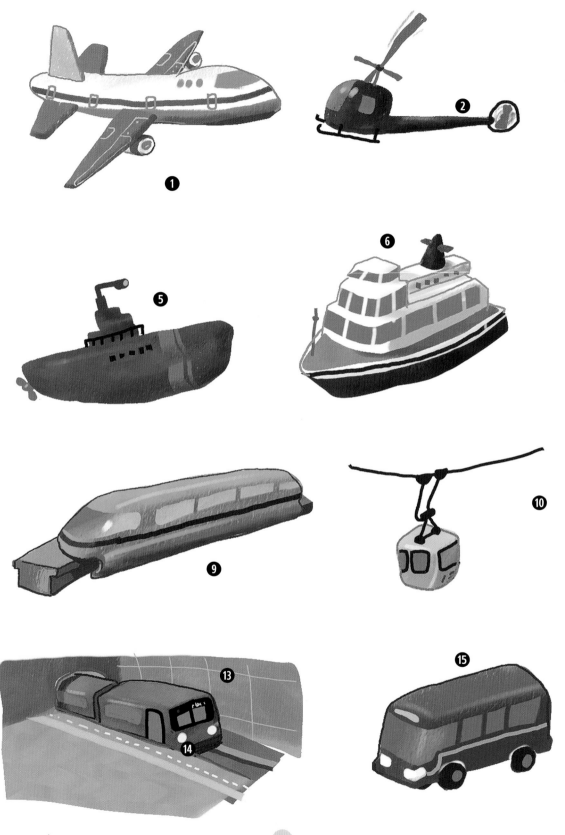

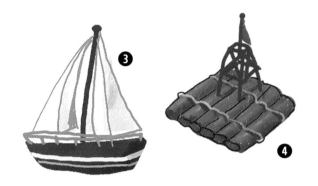

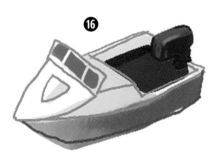

① ジャンボジェット機
6 [janbojettoki] jumbo jet

② ヘリコプター
3 [herikoputâ] helicopter

③ ヨット
1 [yotto] sailboat

④ いかだ
0 [ikada] raft

⑤ 潜水艦
0 [sensuikan] submarine

⑥ フェリー
1 [ferî] ferry

⑦ タクシー
1 [takusî] taxi

⑧ 二階建てバス
6 [nikaidatebasu] double-decker bus

⑨ モノレール
3 [monorêru] monorail

⑩ ロープウェー
4 [rôpuwê] cable car

⑪ 自転車
2 0 [jitensha] bicycle

⑫ オートバイ
3 [ôtobai] scooter

⑬ 電車
0 1 [densha] electric train

⑭ 地下鉄
0 [chikatetsu] subway

⑮ バス
1 [basu] tour bus

⑯ モーターボート
5 [môtâbôto] motorboat

1 歩道橋
0 [hodôkyô] pedestrian bridge

2 角
1 [kado] corner

3 道路標識
4 [dourohyôshiki] street sign

4 地下鉄入り口
0 [chikatetsuiriguchi] subway entrance

5 バス停
0 [basutei] bus stop

6 ガソリンスタンド
6 [gasorinsutando] gas station

7 高速道路
5 [kôsokudôro] freeway

8 大通り
3 [ôdôri] road

9 横断歩道
5 [ôdanhodô] crosswalk

10 交差点
0 3 [kôsaten] intersection

11 街灯
0 [gaitô] streetlight

12 信号
0 [singô] traffic light

13 歩道
0 [hodô] sidewalk

14 地下道
2 [chikadô] underpass

15 パーキングエリア
6 [pâkingueria] parking space

❶ お手洗い
<ruby>手<rt>て</rt></ruby><ruby>洗<rt>あら</rt></ruby>
3 [otearai] lavatory

❷ 乗務員
<ruby>乗<rt>じょう</rt></ruby><ruby>務<rt>む</rt></ruby><ruby>員<rt>いん</rt></ruby>
3 [jômuin] flight attendant

❸ 非常口
<ruby>非<rt>ひ</rt></ruby><ruby>常<rt>じょう</rt></ruby><ruby>口<rt>ぐち</rt></ruby>
2 [hijôguchi] emergency exit

❹ ブラインド
0 [buraindo] window blind

❺ トレー
2 [torê] tray

❻ 救命胴衣
<ruby>救<rt>きゅう</rt></ruby><ruby>命<rt>めい</rt></ruby><ruby>胴<rt>どう</rt></ruby><ruby>衣<rt>い</rt></ruby>
5 [kyumeidôi] life preserver

❼ 窓際の席
<ruby>窓<rt>まど</rt></ruby><ruby>際<rt>ぎわ</rt></ruby>の<ruby>席<rt>せき</rt></ruby>
6 [madogiwanoseki] window seat

❽ 通路側の席
<ruby>通<rt>つう</rt></ruby><ruby>路<rt>ろ</rt></ruby><ruby>側<rt>がわ</rt></ruby>の<ruby>席<rt>せき</rt></ruby>
7 [tsûrogawanoseki] aisle seat

❾ シートベルト
4 [sîtoberuto] seat belt

❿ 副操縦士
<ruby>副<rt>ふく</rt></ruby><ruby>操<rt>そう</rt></ruby><ruby>縦<rt>じゅう</rt></ruby><ruby>士<rt>し</rt></ruby>
5 [fukusôjûsi] copilot

⓫ キャプテン
1 [kyaputen] captain

⓬ ジェットエンジン
4 [jettoenjin] jet engine

⓭ ファーストクラス
5 [fâsutokurasu] first class

⓮ ビジネスクラス
5 [bijinesukurasu] business class

⓯ エコノミークラス
6 [ekonomîkurasu] economy class

❶ ターミナル
1 [tâminaru]
terminal

❷ 自動券売機<ruby>じどうけんばいき</ruby>
6 [jidôkenbaiki]
ticket machine

❸ 両替所<ruby>りょうがえじょ</ruby>
4 [ryôgaesho]
exchange counter

❹ 保険カウンター<ruby>ほけん</ruby>
4 [hokenkauntâ]
insurance counter

❺ 搭乗手続き<ruby>とうじょうてつづ</ruby>
6 [tôjôtetsuzuki]
airport check-in

❻ 旅客<ruby>りょかく</ruby>
0 [ryokaku]
passenger

❼ 航空会社<ruby>こうくうがいしゃ</ruby>
5 [kôkûgaisha]
airline company

❽ 案内係<ruby>あんないがかり</ruby>
5 [annaigakari]
airline representative

❾ 荷物<ruby>にもつ</ruby>
1 [nimotsu]
luggage

❿ 手押車<ruby>ておしくるま</ruby>
4 [teosiguruma]
luggage cart

⓫ 税関<ruby>ぜいかん</ruby>
0 [zeikan]
customs

⓬ 出入国<ruby>しゅつにゅうこく</ruby>
3 [shutsunyukoku]
immigration

⑬ ベルトコンベヤー
<small>6</small> [berutokonbeya]
luggage carousel

⑭ <small>あんないじょ</small>案内所
<small>50</small> [annaijo]
information desk

⑮ <small>しゅっぱつ</small>出発ロビー
<small>5</small> [shuppatsurobi]
departure lobby

⑯ <small>めんぜいひん</small>免税品
<small>30</small> [menzeihin]
duty-free item

⑰ <small>めんぜいてん</small>免税店
<small>3</small> [menzeiten]
duty-free shop

⑱ <small>かんせいとう</small>管制塔
<small>0</small> [kanseitô]
control tower

⑲ <small>りりく</small>離陸
<small>0</small> [ririku]
takeoff

⑳ リムジン
<small>1</small> [rimujin]
shuttle bus

㉑ <small>ちゃくりく</small>着陸
<small>0</small> [chakuriku]
land

㉒ <small>かっそうろ</small>滑走路
<small>3</small> [kassôro]
runway

1

2

5

6

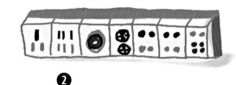

7

9

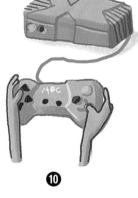

10

11

❶ トランプ
₀ [toranpu] to play cards

❷ 麻雀 ^{マージャン}
₀ [mâjan] to play mahjong

❸ ハイキング
₁ [haikingu] to go hiking

❹ カラオケ
₀ [karaoke] to sing karaoke

❺ ショッピング
₁ ₀ [shoppingu] to window shop

❻ 読書 ^{どくしょ}
₁ [dokusho] to read

❼ 音楽 [～ を聴く] ^{おんがく} ^き
₁ [ongaku] to listen to music

❽ テレビ [～ を見る] ^み
₁ [terebi] to watch TV

❾ 映画 ^{えいが}
₁ ₀ [eiga] to watch movies

❿ テレビゲーム [～ をする]
₄ [terebigêmu] to play video games

⓫ ネットサーフィン
₄ [nettosâfin] to surf the net

⓬ ドライブ
₂ [doraibu] driving

4

8

12

❶ 囲碁
_い_ご
1 [igo] go game

❷ 将棋
_{しょう}_ぎ
0 [shôgi] Japanese chess

❸ チェス
1 [chesu] chess

❹ 踊り
_{おど}
0 [odori] dancing

❺ 釣り
_つ
0 [tsuri] fishing

❻ ガーデニング
0 [gâdeningu] gardening

❼ バードウォッチング
4 [bâdowocchingu] bird-watching

❽ 撮影
_{さつ}_{えい}
0 [satsuei] photography

❾ 彫刻
_{ちょう}_{こく}
0 [chôkoku] sculpture

❿ 絵画
_{かい}_が
1 [kaiga] painting

⓫ 洋裁
_{よう}_{さい}
0 [yôsai] dressmaking

⓬ ヨーガ
1 [yôga] yoga

❶ 救急車^{きゅうきゅうしゃ}
3 [kyûkyûsha]
ambulance

❷ 病室^{びょうしつ}
0 [byôsitsu]
patient's room

❸ 病人^{びょうにん}
0 [byônin]
patient

❹ 診察^{しんさつ}
0 [sinsatsu]
medical examination

❺ 歯科医^{しかい}
2 [sikai]
dentist

❻ 小児科^{しょうにか}
0 [shônika]
pediatrics

❼ 患者^{かんじゃ}
0 [kanja]
patient

❽ 治療^{ちりょう}
0 [chiryô]
treatment

❾ 待合室^{まちあいしつ}
3 [machiaisitsu]
waiting room

❿ 高熱^{こうねつ}
0 [kônetsu]
high fever

⓫ 風邪^{かぜ}
0 [kaze]
cold

⓬ 咳^{せき}
2 [seki]
cough

⓭ 目眩^{めまい}
2 [memai]
dizziness

⓮ 胃痛^{いつう}
0 [itsû]
stomachache

⓯ 頭痛^{ずつう}
0 [zutsû]
headache

16 杖
_{つえ}
1 [tsue]
crutch

17 手術
_{しゅじゅつ}
1 [shujutsu]
operation

18 集中治療室
_{しゅうちゅうちりょうしつ}
6 [shûchûchiryôsitsu]
intensive care unit

19 産婦人科
_{さんふじんか}
6 [sânfujinka]
obstetrics and
gynecology

20 妊婦
_{にんぷ}
1 [ninpu]
pregnant woman

21 医者
_{いしゃ}
0 [isha]
doctor

22 ナースステーション
5 [nâsusutêshon]
nurse station

23 看護婦
_{かんごふ}
3 [kangofu]
nurse

24 歩行器
_{ほこうき}
2 [hokôki]
walker

25 車椅子
_{くるまいす}
3 [kurumaisu]
wheelchair

26 担架
_{たんか}
1 [tanka]
stretcher

27 救急室
_{きゅうきゅうしつ}
3 [kyûkyûsitsu]
emergency room

10 · At the Hospital

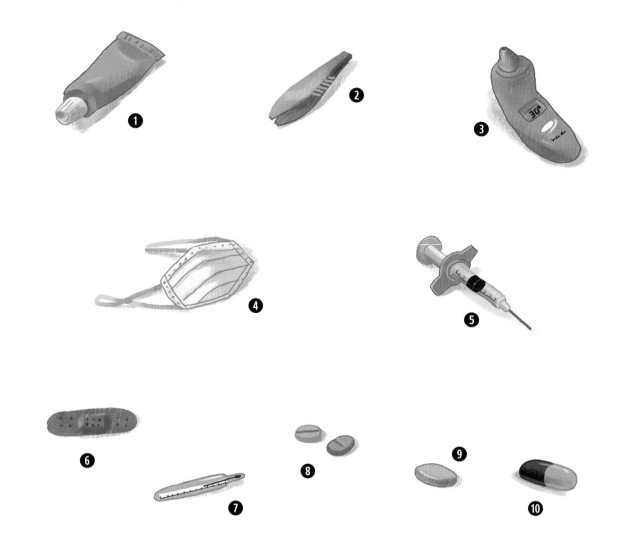

① 軟膏
0 [nankô]
ointment

② ピンセット
3 [pinsetto]
tweezers

③ 耳式体温計
5 [mimisikitaionkei]
ear thermometer

④ マスク
1 [masuku]
gauze mask

⑤ 注射器
3 [chûshaki]
syringe

⑥ 絆創膏
0 [bansôkô]
adhesive bandage

⑦ 体温計
0 3 [taionkei]
clinical thermometer

⑧ 錠剤
0 [jôzai]
tablet

⑨ 丸薬
0 [ganyaku]
pill

⑩ カプセル
1 [kapuseru]
capsule

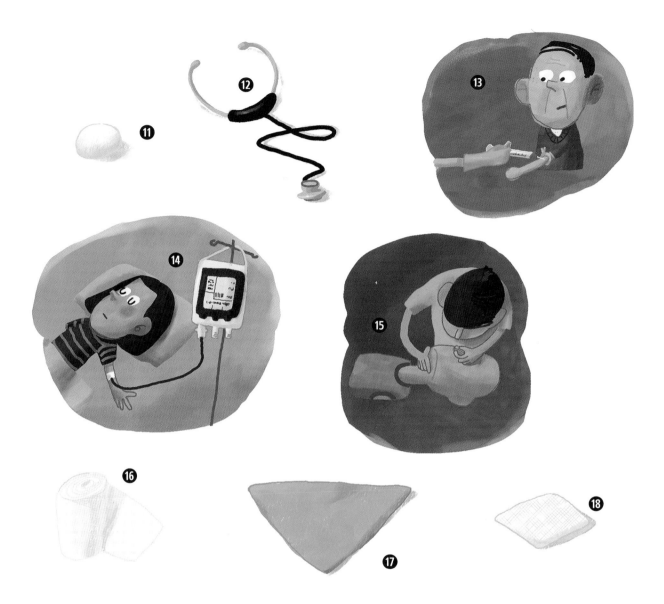

⑪ タンポン
1 [tanpon]
tampon

⑫ 聴診器
　ちょうしんき
3 [chôsinki]
stethoscope

⑬ 採血
　さいけつ
0 [saiketsu]
drawing blood

⑭ 輸血
　ゆけつ
0 [yuketsu]
blood transfusion

⑮ 心肺蘇生法
　しんぱいそせいほう
0 [sinpaisoseihô]
CPR

⑯ 包帯
　ほうたい
0 [hôtai]
bandage

⑰ つり包帯
　　　ほうたい
3 [tsurihôtai]
sling

⑱ ガーゼ
1 [gâze]
gauze

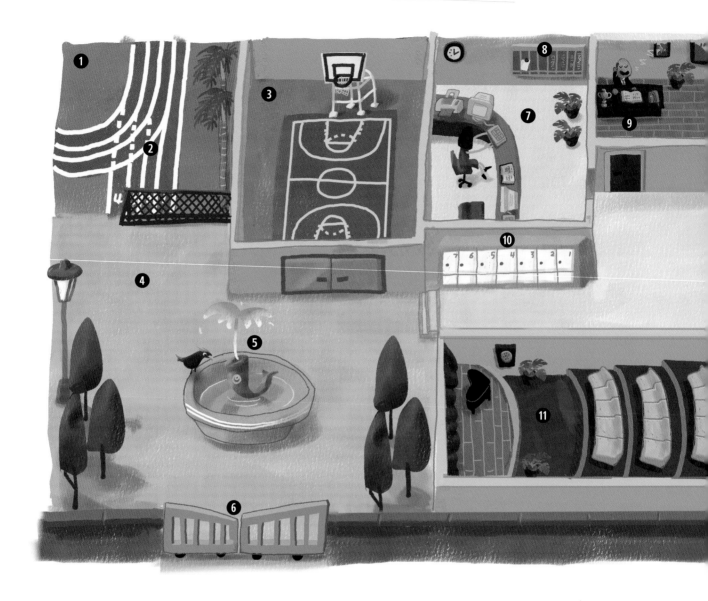

❶ <ruby>運動場<rt>うんどうじょう</rt></ruby>
0 [undôjô]
field

❷ トラック
2 [torakku]
track

❸ バスケットコート
0 [basukettokôto]
basketball court

❹ <ruby>校庭<rt>こうてい</rt></ruby>
0 [kôtei]
schoolyard

❺ <ruby>噴水<rt>ふんすい</rt></ruby>
0 [funsui]
fountain

❻ <ruby>校門<rt>こうもん</rt></ruby>
0 [kômon]
school gate

❼ <ruby>事務室<rt>じむしつ</rt></ruby>
2 [jimusitsu]
office

❽ <ruby>掲示板<rt>けいじばん</rt></ruby>
0 [keijiban]
bulletin board

❾ <ruby>校長室<rt>こうちょうしつ</rt></ruby>
3 [kôchôsitsu]
principal's office

❿ ロッカー
1 [rokkâ]
lockers

⓫ <ruby>講堂<rt>こうどう</rt></ruby>
0 [kôdô]
auditorium

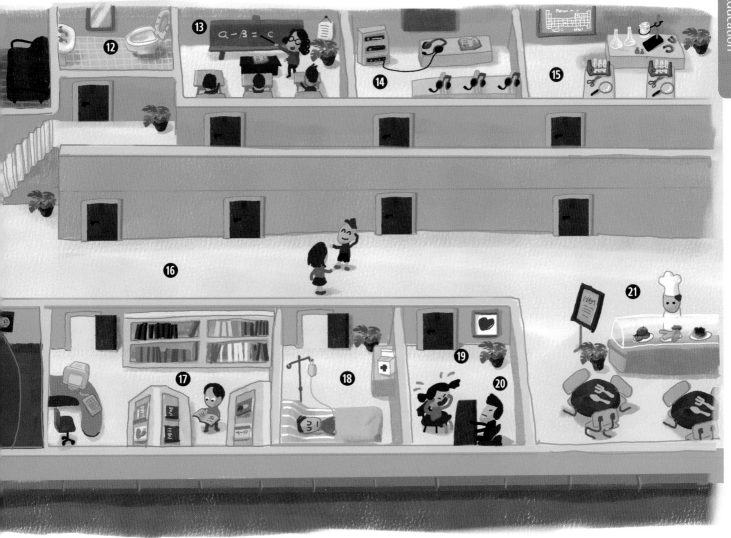

⑫ トイレ
1 [toire]
restroom

きょうしつ
⑬ 教室
0 [kyôsitsu]
classroom

し ちょうかくきょうしつ
⑭ 視聴覚教室
6 [sichôkakukyôsitsu]
language lab

か がくじっしゅうしつ
⑮ 化学実習室
6 [kagakujisshûsitsu]
chemistry lab

ろう か
⑯ 廊下
0 [rôka]
hallway

と しょかん
⑰ 図書館
2 [toshokan]
library

ほ けんしつ
⑱ 保健室
2 [hokensitsu]
nurse's office

そうだんしつ
⑲ 相談室
5 [sôdansitsu]
guidance
counselor's office

きょう し
⑳ 教師
1 [kyôsi]
teacher

㉑ カフェテリア
3 [kafeteria]
cafeteria

❶ 黒板
　0 [kokuban] chalkboard

❷ 時間割
　0 [jikanwari] timetable

❸ 黒板消し
　3 [kokubankesi] eraser

❹ チョーク
　1 [chôku] chalk

❺ マイク
　1 [maiku] microphone

❻ 下敷
　0 [sitajiki] desk pad

❼ 筆箱
　0 [fudebako] pencil box

❽ 机
　0 [tsukue] desk

❾ 放送装置
　5 [hôsôsôchi] broadcaster

❿ 地球儀
　2 [chikyûgi] globe

⓫ プロジェクター
　3 [purojekutâ] projector

⓬ 教科書
　3 [kyôkasho] textbook

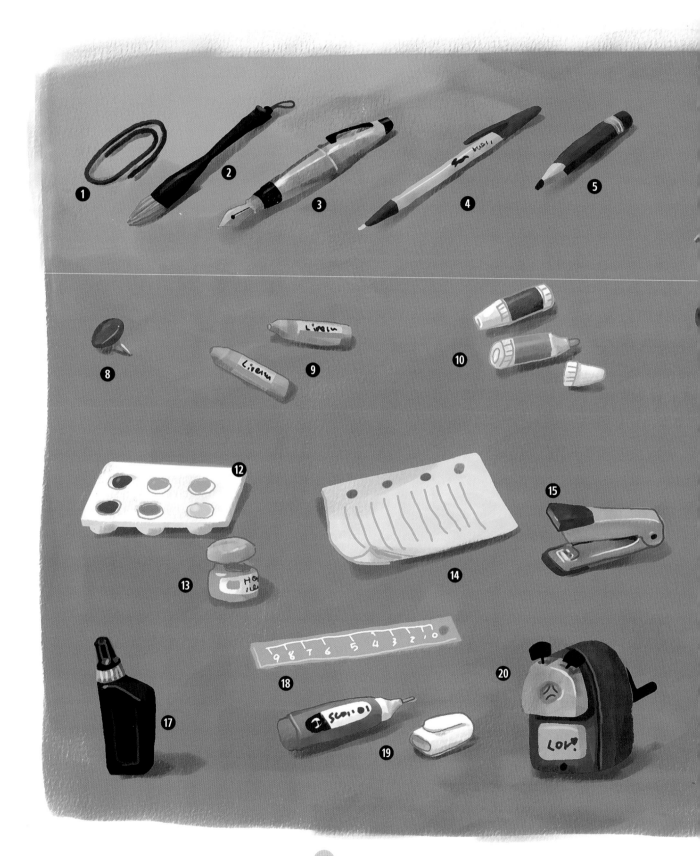

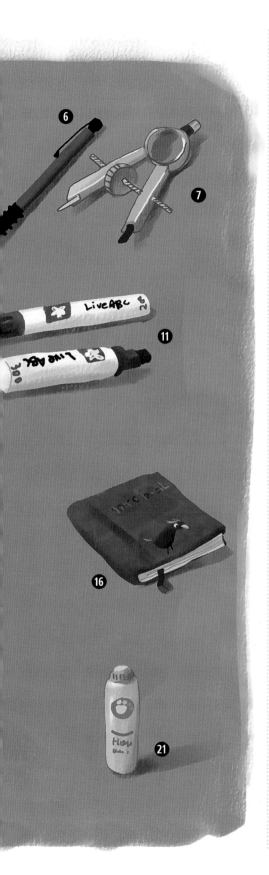

1 クリップ
1 2 [kurippu]
paperclip

2 筆 (ふで)
0 [fude]
calligraphy brush

3 万年筆 (まんねんひつ)
3 [mannenhitsu]
fountain pen

4 ボールペン
4 0 [bôrupen]
ballpoint pen

5 鉛筆 (えんぴつ)
0 [enpitsu]
pencil

6 シャープペンシル
4 [shâpupensiru]
mechanical pencil

7 コンパス
1 [konpasu]
compass

8 画鋲 (が びょう)
0 [gabyô]
thumbtack

9 クレヨン
2 [kureyon]
crayon

10 サインペン
4 [sainpen]
color pen

11 マーカー
0 [mâkâ]
marker

12 パレット
2 1 [paretto]
paint palette

13 絵の具 (え ぐ)
0 [enogu]
paint

14 ルーズリーフ
4 [rûzurîfu]
loose leaf

15 ホッチキス
1 [hocchikisu]
stapler

16 ノート
1 [nôto]
notebook

17 墨汁 (ぼくじゅう)
0 [bokujyû]
ink

18 ものさし
3 4 [monosasi]
ruler

19 修正液 (しゅうせいえき)
3 [shûseieki]
white-out

20 鉛筆削り (えんぴつけずり)
5 [enpitsukezuri]
pencil sharpener

21 のり
0 [nori]
glue

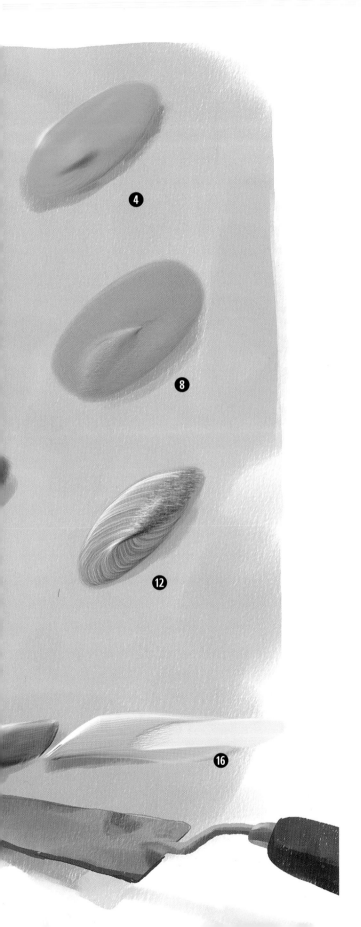

❶ 赤
あか
1 [aka] red

❷ オレンジ色
いろ
0 [orenjiiro] orange

❸ 黄色
き いろ
0 [kiiro] yellow

❹ 緑色
みどりいろ
0 [midoriir] green

❺ 水色
みず いろ
0 [mizuiro] light blue

❻ 青
あお
1 [ao] blue

❼ 紫色
むらさきいろ
0 [murasakirro] purple

❽ ピンク
1 [pinku] pink

❾ 白
しろ
1 [siro] white

❿ 黒
くろ
1 [kuro] black

⓫ 灰色
はいいろ
0 [haiiro] gray

⓬ 銀色
ぎんいろ
0 [giniro] silver

⓭ 金色
きんいろ
0 [kiniro] gold

⓮ 茶色
ちゃいろ
0 [chairo] brown

⓯ 濃い緑
こ みどり
1 [koimidori] dark green

⓰ 薄い緑
うす みどり
4 [usuimidori] light green

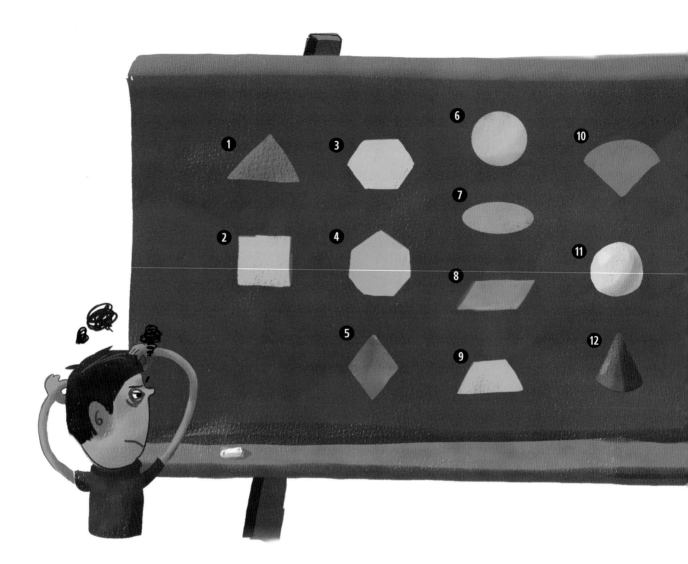

❶ 三角形 さんかくけい
3 4 [sankakukei]
triangle

❷ 四角形 しかくけい
2 3 [sikakukei]
rectangle

❸ 六角形 ろっかくけい
3 4 [rokkakukei]
hexagon

❹ 多角形 たかくけい
2 3 [takakukei]
polygon

❺ 菱形 ひしがた
0 [hisigata]
diamond

❻ 円形 えんけい
0 [enkei]
circle

❼ 楕円形 だえんけい
0 [daenkei]
oval

❽ 平行四辺形 へいこうしへんけい
6 [heikôsihenkei]
parallelogram

❾ 台形 だいけい
0 [daikei]
trapezoid

❿ 扇形 おうぎがた
0 [ôgigata]
sector

⓫ 球形 きゅうけい
0 [kyûkei]
sphere

⓬ 円錐 えんすい
0 [ensui]
cone

⓭ プラス
0 1 [purasu]
plus sign

⓮ マイナス
0 [mainasu]
minus sign

⑮ 倍
<ruby>倍<rt>ばい</rt></ruby>
0 [bai]
multiplication sign

⑯ 割る
<ruby>割<rt>わ</rt></ruby>る
0 [waru]
division sign

⑰ 等しい
<ruby>等<rt>ひと</rt></ruby>しい
3 [hitosî]
equals sign

⑱ 計算
<ruby>計<rt>けい</rt>算<rt>さん</rt></ruby>
0 [keisan]
calculation

⑲ 足し算
<ruby>足<rt>た</rt></ruby>し<ruby>算<rt>ざん</rt></ruby>
2 [tasizan]
addition

⑳ 引き算
<ruby>引<rt>ひ</rt></ruby>き<ruby>算<rt>ざん</rt></ruby>
2 [hikizan]
subtraction

㉑ 掛け算
<ruby>掛<rt>か</rt></ruby>け<ruby>算<rt>ざん</rt></ruby>
2 [kakezan]
multiplication

㉒ 割り算
<ruby>割<rt>わ</rt></ruby>り<ruby>算<rt>ざん</rt></ruby>
2 [warizen]
division

㉓ 平方
<ruby>平<rt>へい</rt>方<rt>ほう</rt></ruby>
0 [heihô]
square

㉔ 平方根
<ruby>平<rt>へい</rt>方<rt>ほう</rt>根<rt>こん</rt></ruby>
3 [heihôkon]
square root symbol

㉕ 分数
<ruby>分<rt>ぶん</rt>数<rt>すう</rt></ruby>
3 [bunsû]
fraction

㉖ 二分の一
<ruby>二<rt>に</rt>分<rt>ぶん</rt></ruby>の<ruby>一<rt>いち</rt></ruby>
0 [nibunnoichi]
half

❶ スカイダイビング
4 [sukaidaibingu]
skydiving

❷ ボート
1 [bôto]
boating

❸ フィギュアスケート
5 [figyuasukêto]
figure skating

❹ アイススケート
5 [aisusukêto]
ice-skating

❺ ジョギング
0 [jogingu]
jogging

❻ ローラースケート
6 [rôrâsukêto]
roller skating

❼ インラインスケート
7 [inrainsukêto]
in-line skating

❽ ラフティング
3 [rafuthingu]
rafting

❾ サイクリング
4 [saikuringu]
cycling

⑩ スケートボード
5 [sukêtobôdo]
skateboarding

⑪ ハンググライディング
7 [hanguguraidhingu]
hang gliding

⑫ 乗馬 (じょうば)
0 [jôba]
horseback riding

⑬ 弓術 (きゅうじゅつ)
0 1 [kyûjutsu]
archery

⑭ スノーボード
4 [sunôbôdo]
snowboarding

⑮ スキー
2 [sukî]
skiing

⑯ ロッククライミング
5 [rokkukuraimingu]
rock climbing

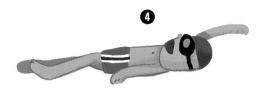

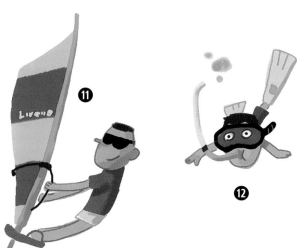

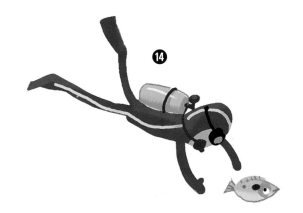

❶ 犬かき
_{いぬ}
3 [inukaki] dog paddle

❷ 平泳ぎ
_{ひら およ}
3 [hiraoyogi] breaststroke

❸ 自由形
_{じ ゆうがた}
0 [jiyûgata] freestyle

❹ 背泳ぎ
_{せ およ}
2 [seoyogi] backstroke

❺ バタフライ
1 3 [batafurai] butterfly stroke

❻ 横泳ぎ
_{よこ およ}
3 [yokooyogi] sidestroke

❼ ダイビング
1 0 [daibingu] to dive

❽ シンクロナイズドスイミング
9 [sinkuronaizudosuimingu]
synchronized swimming

❾ 水上スキー
_{すい じょう}
5 [suijôsukî] waterskiing

❿ サーフィン
1 0 [sâfin] surfing

⓫ ウインドサーフィン
5 [uindosâfin] windsurfing

⓬ シュノーケル
2 [shunôkeru] snorkeling

⓭ 水上オートバイ
_{すい じょう}
7 [suijôôtobai] jet skiing

⓮ 潜水
_{せん すい}
0 [sensui] scuba diving

❶ 走り幅跳び
4 [hasirihabatobi]
long jump

❷ ハンマー投げ
0 [hanmanage]
hammer throw

❸ 障害物競走
7 [shôgaibutsukyôsô]
steeplechase

❹ マラソン
0 [marason]
marathon

❺ リレー
0 [rirê]
relay race

❻ 走り高跳び
4 5 [hasiritakatobi]
high jump

❼ 棒高跳び
3 4 [bôtakatobi]
pole vault

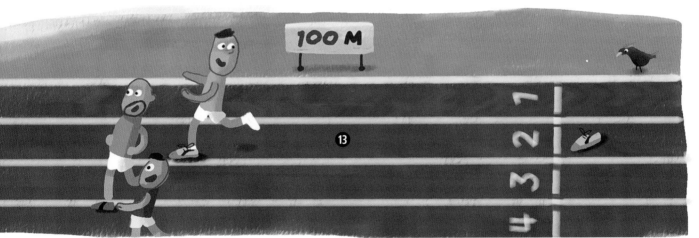

❽ 槍投げ
　や り な
0 [yarinage]
javelin throw

❾ ハードル競走
　　　　きょうそう
5 [hâdorukyôsô]
hurdles

❿ 三段跳び
　さ ん だ ん と
0 [sandantobi]
triple jump

⓫ 円盤投げ
　え ん ば ん な
0 [enbannage]
discus throw

⓬ 短距離レース
　た ん き ょ り
5 [tankyorirêsu]
sprint

⓭ 百メートル競走
　ひゃく　　　　　きょうそう
7 [hyakumêtorukyôsô]
hundred-meter dash

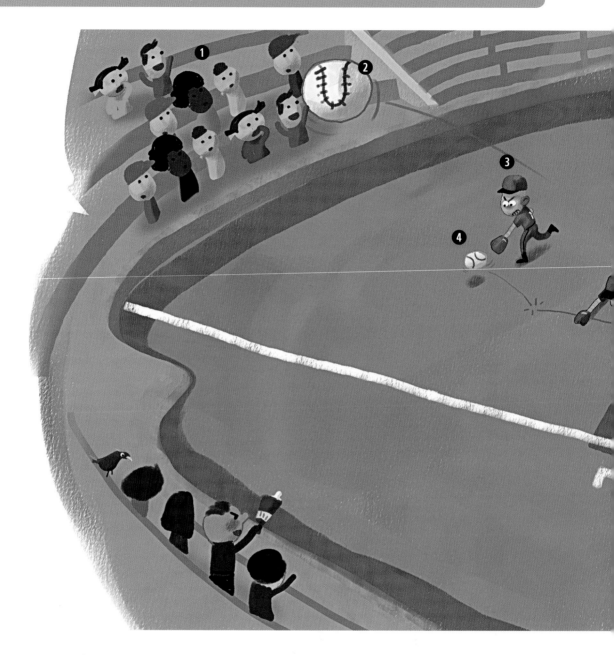

❶ バックスタンド
5 [bakkusutando]
bleacher

❷ ホームラン
3 [hômuran]
home run

❸ レフト
1 [refuto]
left fielder

❹ ヒット
1 [hitto]
hit

❺ ショート
1 [shôto]
shortstop

❻ センター
1 [sentâ]
center fielder

❼ ライト
1 [raito]
right fielder

❽ 外野（がいや）
0 [gaiya]
outfield

❾ グローブ
2 [gurôbu]
glove

❿ ベース
1 [bêsu]
base

⓫ セカンド
0 [sekando]
second baseman

⓬ サード
1 [sâdo]
third baseman

⑬ ファースト
0 [fâsuto]
first baseman

⑭ ピッチャー
1 [picchâ]
pitcher

⑮ マウンド
0 [maundo]
mound

⑯ ユニフォーム
3 [yunihômu]
uniform

⑰ 内野
<ruby>内野<rt>ない や</rt></ruby>
0 [naiya]
infield

⑱ バッターボックス
5 [battâbokkusu]
batter's box

⑲ バッター
1 [battâ]
hitter

⑳ バット
1 [batto]
bat

㉑ 背番号
<ruby>背番号<rt>せ ばんごう</rt></ruby>
2 [sebangô]
player number

㉒ ホームベース
4 [hômubêsu]
home plate

㉓ キャッチャー
1 [kyacchâ]
catcher

㉔ 球審
<ruby>球審<rt>きゅうしん</rt></ruby>
0 [kyûsin]
umpire

❶ ねずみ
0 [nezumi]
mouse

❷ 犬（いぬ）
2 [inu]
dog

❸ やぎ
1 [yagi]
goat

❹ 牛（うし）
0 [usi]
cattle

❺ 猫（ねこ）
1 [neko]
cat

❻ 豚（ぶた）
0 [buta]
pig

❼ 羊（ひつじ）
0 [hitsuji]
sheep

❽ ろば
1 [roba]
donkey

❾ うさぎ
0 [usagi]
rabbit

❿ 猿（さる）
1 [saru]
monkey

⓫ りす
1 [risu]
squirrel

⓬ コアラ
1 [koara]
koala

⓭ しまうま
0 [simauma]
zebra

⓮ きりん
0 [kirin]
giraffe

⓯ カンガルー
3 [kangarû]
kangaroo

⓰ こうもり
1 [kômori]
bat

⑰ 蛇
へび
1 [hebi]
snake

⑱ 鹿
しか
0 2 [sika]
deer

⑲ 狼
おおかみ
1 [ôkami]
wolf

⑳ らくだ
0 [rakuda]
camel

㉑ 白熊
しろくま
0 [sirokuma]
polar bear

㉒ 狐
きつね
0 [kitsune]
fox

㉓ サイ
1 [sai]
rhinoceros

㉔ 馬
うま
2 [uma]
horse

㉕ パンダ
1 [panda]
panda

㉖ かば
1 [kaba]
hippopotamus

㉗ 熊
くま
2 [kuma]
brown bear

㉘ ライオン
0 [raion]
lion

㉙ 象
ぞう
1 [zô]
elephant

㉚ とら
0 [tora]
tiger

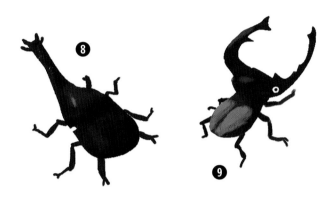

❶ ハエ
0 [hae] fly

❷ 蚊
0 [ka] mosquito

❸ ゴキブリ
0 [gokiburi] cockroach

❹ 蜂
0 [hachi] bee

❺ 蝉
0 [semi] cicada

❻ 蛍
1 [hotaru] firefly

❼ てんとうむし
3 [tentômusi] ladybug

❽ かぶとむし
3 [kabutomusi] rhinoceros beetle

❾ くわがたむし
4 [kuwagatamusi] stag beetle

❿ とんぼ
0 [tonbo] dragonfly

⓫ 蝶
1 [chô] butterfly

⓬ こおろぎ
1 [kôrogi] cricket

⓭ あり
0 [ari] ant

⓮ 蛾
0 [ga] moth

⓯ のみ
2 [nomi] flea

⓰ かまきり
1 [kamakiri] praying mantis

❶ かもめ
0 [kamome]
seagull

❷ ペンギン
0 [pengin]
penguin

❸ はと
1 [hato]
pigeon

❹ からす
1 [karasu]
crow

❺ 鴨
1 [kamo]
duck

❻ すずめ
0 [suzume]
sparrow

❼ キツツキ
2 [kitsutsuki]
woodpecker

❽ カナリア
0 [kanaria]
canary

❾ ひばり
0 [hibari]
lark

❿ はちどり
2 [hachidori]
hummingbird

⓫ つばめ
0 [tsubame]
swallow

⑫ **がちょう**
0 [gachô]
goose

⑬ **たか**
0 [taka]
eagle

⑭ **ふくろう**
2 3 [fukurô]
owl

⑮ **白鳥**
はくちゅう
0 [hakuchô]
swan

⑯ **鶴**
つる
1 [tsuru]
crane

⑰ **孔雀**
く じゃく
0 [kujaku]
peacock

⑱ **オウム**
0 [oumu]
parrot

⑲ **七面鳥**
しちめんちょう
0 [sichimenchô]
turkey

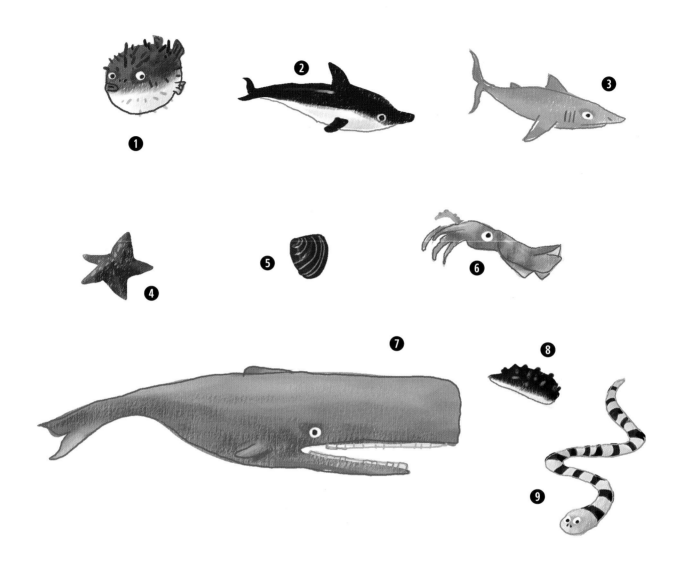

① ふぐ
1 [fugu]
blowfish

② いるか
0 [iruka]
dolphin

③ さめ
0 [same]
shark

④ ひとで
0 [hitode]
starfish

⑤ はまぐり
2 [hamaguri]
clam

⑥ やりいか
2 0 [yariika]
squid

⑦ 鯨
0 [kujira]
whale

⑧ なまこ
3 0 [namako]
sea cucumber

⑨ ウミヘビ
0 [umihebi]
sea snake

⑩ タツノオトシゴ
0 6 [tatsunootosigo]
sea horse

⑪ 珊瑚
さんご
1 [sango]
coral

⑫ 海草
かいそう
2 0 [kaisô]
seaweed

⑬ 蟹
かに
0 [kani]
crab

⑭ 海亀
うみがめ
0 [umigame]
sea turtle

⑮ たこ
1 [tako]
octopus

⑯ くらげ
0 [kurage]
jellyfish

⑰ アザラシ
2 [azarasi]
seal

⑱ ロブスター
2 [robusutâ]
lobster

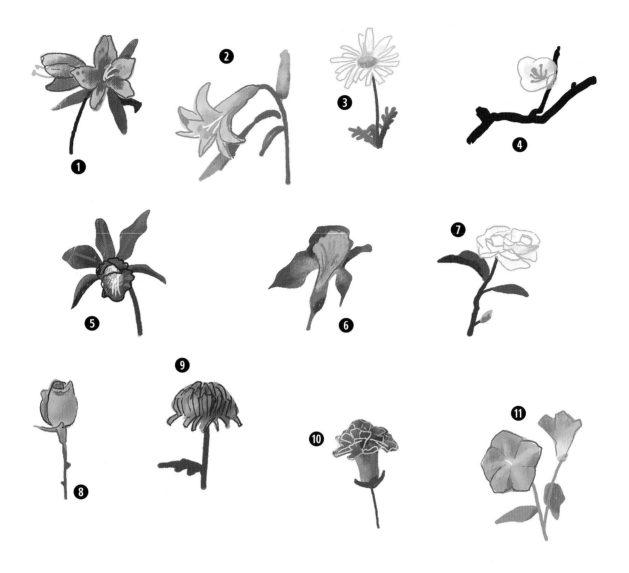

1 つつじ
0 2 [tsutsuji]
azalea

2 ゆり
0 [yuri]
lily

3 雛菊
2 [hinagiku]
daisy

4 梅
0 [ume]
plum blossom

5 蘭
1 [ran]
orchid

6 アヤメ
0 [ayame]
iris

7 椿
1 [tsubaki]
camellia

8 薔薇
0 [bara]
rose

9 菊
2 [kiku]
chrysanthemum

10 カーネーション
3 [kânêshon]
carnation

11 あさがお
2 [asagao]
morning glory

12

13

14

15

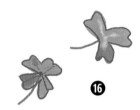

16

17

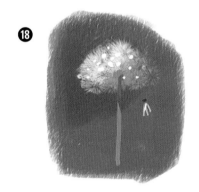

18

19

12 ラベンダー
2 [rabendâ]
lavender

13 ひまわり
2 [himawari]
sunflower

14 チューリップ
1 3 [chûrippu]
tulip

15 スミレ
0 [sumire]
violet

16 カタバミ
0 [katabami]
shamrock

17 ポインセチア
4 [poinsechia]
poinsettia

18 タンポポ
1 [tanpopo]
dandelion

19 桜
さくら
0 [sakura]
cherry blossom

❶

❷

❸

❹

❺

❻

❼

❽

❾

❿

⓫

⓬

❶ 一月
　⁴ [ichigatsu]
　January

❷ 二月
　³ [nigatsu]
　February

❸ 三月
　¹ [sangatsu]
　March

❹ 四月
　³ [sigatsu]
　April

❺ 五月
　¹ [gogatsu]
　May

❻ 六月
　⁴ [rokugatsu]
　June

❼ 七月
　⁴ [sichigatsu]
　July

❽ 八月
　⁴ [hachigatsu]
　August

❾ 九月
　¹ [kugatsu]
　September

❿ 十月
　⁴ [jûgatsu]
　October

⓫ 十一月
　⁶ [jûichigatsu]
　November

⓬ 十二月
　⁵ [jûnigatsu]
　December

⑬ 日曜日
にちようび
3 [nichiyôbi]
Sunday

⑭ 月曜日
げつようび
3 [getsuyôbi]
Monday

⑮ 火曜日
かようび
2 [kayôbi]
Tuesday

⑯ 水曜日
すいようび
3 [suiyôbi]
Wednesday

⑰ 木曜日
もくようび
3 [mokuyôbi]
Thursday

⑱ 金曜日
きんようび
3 [kinyôbi]
Friday

⑲ 土曜日
どようび
2 [doyôbi]
Saturday

⑳ 祝祭日
しゅくさいじつ
3 [shukusaijitsu]
national holiday

14 · Daily Life

① 太陽
1 [taiyô]
sun

② 雲
1 [kumo]
cloud

③ 雨
1 [ame]
rain

④ 風
0 [kaze]
wind

⑤ 雷
3 4 [kaminari]
thunder

⑥ 稲妻
0 [inazuma]
lightning

⑦ 霧
0 [kiri]
fog

⑧ 霜
2 [simo]
frost

⑨ 雪
2 [yuki]
snow

⑩ 嵐
1 [arasi]
storm

⑪ 気温
0 [kion]
temperature

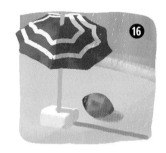

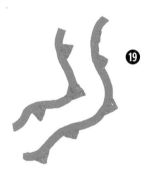

⑫ 台風
<ruby>台風<rt>たいふう</rt></ruby>
3 ［taifû］
typhoon

⑬ 氷
<ruby>氷<rt>こおり</rt></ruby>
0 ［kôri］
ice

⑭ 竜巻
<ruby>竜巻<rt>たつまき</rt></ruby>
0 ［tatsumaki］
tornado

⑮ 春
<ruby>春<rt>はる</rt></ruby>
1 ［haru］
spring

⑯ 夏
<ruby>夏<rt>なつ</rt></ruby>
2 ［natsu］
summer

⑰ 秋
<ruby>秋<rt>あき</rt></ruby>
1 ［aki］
fall/autumn

⑱ 冬
<ruby>冬<rt>ふゆ</rt></ruby>
2 ［fuyu］
winter

⑲ 寒冷前線
<ruby>寒冷前線<rt>かんれいぜんせん</rt></ruby>
5 ［kanreizensen］
cold front

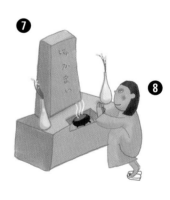

❶ 新年
しんねん
1 [sinnen]
New Year

❷ 初詣
はつもうで
3 [hatsumôde]
New Year's shrine visit

❸ お年玉
としだま
0 [otosidama]
lucky money

❹ 花見
はなみ
0 [hanami]
cherry blossom viewing

❺ 和菓子
わがし
2 [wagasi]
Japanese confectionery

❻ 弁当
べんとう
3 [bentô]
lunch box

❼ 中元
ちゅうげん
0 [chûgen]
15th day of the 7th
lunar month

❽ 墓参り
はかまい
3 [hakamairi]
visit to a grave

❾ 夏祭り
なつまつ
3 [natsumatsuri]
summer festival

❿ 花火
はなび
1 [hanabi]
fireworks

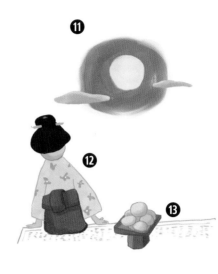

⑪ 中秋
ちゅうしゅう
0 [chûshû]
15th day of the 8th lunar month

⑫ 月見
つきみ
0 [tsukimi]
moon viewing

⑬ 月見団子
つきみだんご
4 [tsukimidango]
tsukimi dango

⑭ クリスマス
3 [kurisumasu]
Christmas
(**クリスマスイブ**
6 [kurisumasuibu]
Christmas Eve)

⑮ クリスマスツリー
7 [kurisumasutsurî]
Christmas tree

⑯ イルミネーション
4 [iruminêshon]
illumination

⑰ お歳暮
せいぼ
0 [oseibo]
end of the year
(year-end gift)

⑱ 大晦日
おおみそか
3 [ômisoka]
New Year's Eve

❶ 高原（こうげん）
⁰ [kôgen]
plateau

❷ 滝（たき）
⁰ [taki]
waterfall

❸ 森（もり）
⁰ [mori]
forest

❹ 湖（みずうみ）
³ [mizuumi]
lake

❺ 峰（みね）
² ¹ [mine]
peak

❻ 山（やま）
² [yama]
mountain

❼ 池（いけ）
² [ike]
pond

❽ 川（かわ）
² [kawa]
river

❾ 川岸（かわぎし）
⁰ [kawagisi]
riverside

❿ 陸（りく）
⁰ ² [riku]
land

⓫ 谷（たに）
² [tani]
valley

132

⑫ 盆地
ぼん ち
0 [bonchi]
basin

⑬ 平原
へいげん
0 [heigen]
plain

⑭ 港
みなと
0 [minato]
harbor

⑮ 海辺
うみ べ
0 3 [umibe]
seashore

⑯ ビーチ
1 [bîchi]
beach

⑰ 水平線
すいへいせん
0 [suiheisen]
horizon

⑱ 島
しま
2 [sima]
island

⑲ 海
うみ
1 [umi]
sea

Index

Index

Index

Index

Index

Index

Index